SITTING BULL
HIS LIFE AND LEGACY

⌒

The hardback edition of this book, first printed in 2009, was the first time the story of Sitting Bull had been written and published by a lineal descendant. Now available in paperback, Ernie LaPointe, a great-grandson of the famous Hunkpapa Lakota chief, presents the family tales and memories told to him about his great-grandfather. In *Sitting Bull: His Life and Legacy*, LaPointe not only recounts the rich oral history of his family—the stories of Sitting Bull's childhood, his reputation as a fierce warrior, his growth into a sage and devoted leader of his people, and the betrayal that led to his murder—but also explains what it means to be Lakota in the time of Sitting Bull and now.

In many ways the oral history differs from what became the standard and widely accepted biography of Sitting Bull. LaPointe explains the discrepancies, how they occurred, and why he chose to tell his story of Tatanka Iyotake. This book is powerful. It is a story of Native American history, told by a Native American, for all people to better understand a culture, a leader, and a man.

Tatanka Iyotake Ta Tiwahe (Sitting Bull's Family)

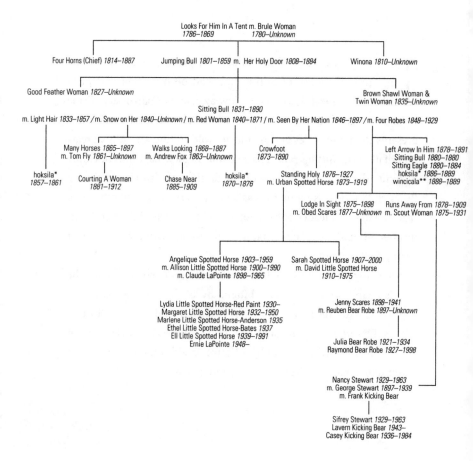

Looks For Him In A Tent m. Brule Woman
1786–1869   1780–Unknown

Four Horns (Chief) 1814–1887   Jumping Bull 1801–1859 m. Her Holy Door 1808–1884   Winona 1810–Unknown

Good Feather Woman 1827–Unknown

Brown Shawl Woman &
Twin Woman 1835–Unknown

Sitting Bull 1831–1890

m. Light Hair 1833–1857 / m. Snow on Her 1840–Unknown / m. Red Woman 1840–1871 / m. Seen By Her Nation 1846–1897 / m. Four Robes 1848–1929

Many Horses 1865–1897
m. Tom Fly 1861–Unknown

Walks Looking 1868–1887
m. Andrew Fox 1863–Unknown

Crowfoot
1873–1890

Left Arrow In Him 1878–1891
Sitting Bull 1880–1880
Sitting Eagle 1880–1884
hoksila* 1886–1889
winicala** 1888–1889

hoksila*
1857–1861

Courting A Woman
1881–1912

Chase Near
1885–1909

hoksila*
1870–1876

Standing Holy 1876–1927
m. Urban Spotted Horse 1873–1919

Lodge In Sight 1875–1898
m. Obed Scares 1877–Unknown

Runs Away From 1878–1909
m. Scout Woman 1875–1931

Angelique Spotted Horse 1903–1959
m. Allison Little Spotted Horse 1900–1990
m. Claude LaPointe 1898–1965

Sarah Spotted Horse 1907–2000
m. David Little Spotted Horse
1910–1975

Lydia Little Spotted Horse-Red Paint 1930–
Margaret Little Spotted Horse 1932–1950
Marlene Little Spotted Horse-Anderson 1935
Ethel Little Spotted Horse-Bates 1937
Ell Little Spotted Horse 1939–1991
Ernie LaPointe 1948–

Jenny Scares 1898–1941
m. Reuben Bear Robe 1897–Unknown

Julia Bear Robe 1921–1934
Raymond Bear Robe 1927–1998

Nancy Stewart 1929–1963
m. George Stewart 1897–1939
m. Frank Kicking Bear

Sifrey Stewart 1929–1963
Lavern Kicking Bear 1943–
Casey Kicking Bear 1936–1984

* unnamed boy
** unnamed girl

SITTING BULL
HIS LIFE AND LEGACY

ERNIE LAPOINTE
GREAT-GRANDSON OF SITTING BULL

GIBBS SMITH
TO ENRICH AND INSPIRE HUMANKIND

First Edition
25 24 23 22   5 4 3 2

Published by
Gibbs Smith
P.O. Box 667
Layton, Utah 84041

Orders: 1.800.835.4993
www.gibbs-smith.com

Designed by Rudy Ramos
Printed and bound in China
Gibbs Smith books are printed on either recycled, 100% post-
consumer waste, FSC-certified papers or on paper produced from a
100% certified sustainable forest/controlled wood source.

Library of Congress Cataloging-in-Publication Data

LaPointe, Ernie.
Sitting Bull : his life and legacy / Ernie LaPointe.
p. cm.
ISBN 978-1-4236-0556-0 (Hardcover)
ISBN 978-1-4236-5798-9 (Paperback)
1. Sitting Bull, 1831–1890. 2. Sitting Bull, 1831–1890—Legends.
3. Dakota Indians—Kings and rulers—Biography. 4. Hunkpapa
Indians—Kings and rulers—Biography. 5. Dakota Indians—Wars.
6. Dakota Indians—Government relations. 7. Oral tradition—South
Dakota—Pine Ridge Indian Reservation. I. Title.
E99.D1.S569 2009
978.004'9752—dc22
[B]
                                        2009004745

For my sister Marlene Andersen—for her steadfast support and love

*For my wife Sonja—for her unconditional love, support,
charisma, and exceptional wisdom*

*And, for my children and grandchildren, so they can
gain an understanding of a Lakota ancestor*

CONTENTS

ACKNOWLEDGMENTS

The following individuals and institutions were graciously kind and generous with their time and knowledge: My late mother Angelique Spotted Horse-LaPointe, my granduncles John Sitting Bull (Refuses Them) and Henry Little Soldier for their oral stories which I wrote down in this book; my sister Marlene Andersen for refreshing my memory; Serle Chapman, a great writer of the real West, who seeks the truth and who provided me with the original photographs; Lani Van Eck, my contributing editor, who persuaded me to put my oral history into book form; Bill Billeck of the Smithsonian Institution in Washington, D.C., who allowed me to publish parts of the report on the repatriation of the lock of hair and the leggings of my great-grandfather; Bill Matson, my friend the moviemaker, who stood behind me with his encouragement during the filming of our DVDs and through the writing times of this book; Bess Edwards, the grandniece of Annie Oakley (Little Sure Shot), who shared a story with me that I included in this book, and I cherish her friendship; Sion Hanson, the great-grandnephew of James Hanson, for sharing his story with me; Sharon Small, curator at the Little Bighorn Battlefield Museum; John Doerner, historian at the Little Bighorn Battlefield; Carol Bainbridge, director at the Fort St. Joseph Museum in Niles, Michigan; the Library of Congress; the Glenbow Museum in Calgary, Canada; Ken Woody and Michael "Bad Hand" Terry, who introduced me to Gibbs Smith. A special thank you to Gibbs, for the royal treatment you gave me. To Michelle Branson, my editor, thanks for your patience. And a big thanks to all the staff at Gibbs Smith. Finally, to my wife Sonja, for creating the family tree, and finding all the documents, legal papers, and official letters to back up my oral story.

Pilamaya Yelo (thank you) to everyone who touched my life and gave me inspiration and direction.

ERNIE LaPOINTE

10

FOREWORD

This is Ernie's story of the life of his great-grandfather. He was initially hesitant about putting this oral history into written form. It was only after long consideration and much urging by a number of people (including me) that he agreed. The most convincing argument I could make was based on the durability of this medium. Books have been a continuous part of human life for thousands of years. Written records last.

In many ways, this is not a conventional biography. Instead, it is a written form of oral history, with all the advantages and difficulties that entails. Oral tradition operates within its own framework of conventions and rhythms, not all of which translate readily. A spoken narrative can make use of a number of dramatic devices that are not available in written form.

Speaking allows the narrator to set a pace, to develop a cadence that carries the listener forward into the action of the story. Altering the tempo subtly creates mood, quickening with excitement or slowing with comfort. Inflection expresses emotional content without the need for further explanation. Tonality trumpets defiance or whispers humility.

Body language comes into play as well. In the Lakota oral tradition, stories are told face to face. The narrator can focus attention on his words through his body's stillness or, through his gestures, enhance and expand the scope of what is communicated. A master of the oral tradition—and Ernie is such a master—is a true performance artist who holds his audience in thrall.

Oral tradition also differs from standard written biography in content. The conventional biography relies on a chronological unfolding of the major events within the lifetime of its subject. Considerable effort is expended in creating an overview and weaving the life of the chronicled individual into this context. Cause and effect, stimulus and response become criteria by which the main character is evaluated, explained, and ultimately judged.

In oral history, the intent is subtly different. Chronology is not as important a consideration, and little attention is devoted to detailing every moment. Instead, the narrative is episodic in its focus, and each episode has a *point*. There are morals to these stories. They are intensely value-laden. Ultimately, a standard biography may convey to its reader a carefully woven tapestry, where each thread is tightly and precisely placed to ensure its accuracy in the overall presentation of a factual picture. An oral history, on the other hand, is more analogous to a well-constructed quilt whose patches of vibrant color work together to create a warm impressionistic pattern.

One of the challenges in writing this book was to merge the two, confining the flow of the spoken narrative within the structure of the written form. Ernie was adamant that nothing be included in this book that is not absolutely and strictly the truth as he knows it and has personally experienced it. This raises the second major complication in creating this written narrative. The truth that Ernie seeks to impart in this work is a Lakota truth.

Ernie is a truly bilingual individual. However, there are still translation problems that arise between Lakota and English. The issue here is conceptual, a question of very different world views. The Lakota perspective on the universe and our human place in it is unlike the beliefs espoused by the surrounding culture of the United States. The distinctions are fundamental and mold the shape of the entire culture.

The understandings of the nature of our being and the purpose of our existence are deeply ingrained in all of us, taught to us from the beginning of our awareness. They form the focal point for our most basic assumptions about life and how we should interact with others. What are worthy goals, and how should we define success?

In the culture of the United States, we are taught to cherish our inalienable rights to "life, liberty, and the pursuit of happiness." These, however, are cultural values which, while critical to our society, may well be subordinate to other values in other cultures. As an example, I could not begin to enumerate the number of times I have heard Ernie stress the values of honor, respect, humbleness, and compassion. When you read this book, you will encounter these core values repeatedly. If you are also a member of the Lakota culture, these values have probably resonated for you at a deeply personal level.

If, like me, you are not Lakota, then your understanding, however empathetic and well-intentioned it may be, will be colored by the values of the culture that taught you your basic assumptions about life. It is this unavoidable fact of existence that leads to so many of our intercultural misunderstandings. Communicating across cultural boundaries is often exceptionally difficult.

In the formative stages of this work, I met and communicated with

Ernie and his wife, Sonja, on a frequent basis. I was able to observe as Ernie's confidence in his ability to tell his great-grandfather's story in writing grew to fruition. This is the product of his mind—but even more important, it is from his heart.

It has been an honor and a privilege for me to take part in this endeavor.

Pilamaya.

DR. LANI VAN ECK
Professor of Anthropology and
Cofounder of Wounded Knee: The Museum

PREFACE

My name is Ernie LaPointe, and my Lakota name is Kangi Sie (Crowfoot). I am one of the four great-grandchildren of Sitting Bull (Tatanka Iyotake). I am writing this book from the family stories—traditional oral history—told to me, my older sister Marlene Andersen, a niece, and a nephew by my mother, Angelique Spotted Horse LaPointe. This book is not a complete biography because I am only retelling the stories my mother told of my great-grandfather. My niece and nephew have made the journey to the Spirit World, and my sister Marlene has given me her power of attorney to settle issues pertaining to our great-grandfather. We are the lineal descendants of Sitting Bull.

The Lakota people believe the number four is sacred in all things. We have pursued four ways of establishing our lineage to Sitting Bull because our family ties are sacred. The first path is through the oral history that is retold in this book. The second is through the paper trail—legal documents, land allotments, enrollment records, birth records, and other tribal documentation. We have used this information to create a thorough, well-documented family tree. The third is through sacred ceremonies when the spirit of our great-grandfather recognized us as his grandchildren during a repatriation ceremony for his leggings and lock of hair. The fourth will be through DNA, the modern concept of identifying relatives from the genetic codes of human beings from the past and present. The DNA testing is currently underway by a specialist in Denmark who primarily focuses on ancient DNA. The testing is difficult because the lock of hair was chemically treated for museum preservation purposes. We expect to have the results of this testing by the end of 2009. It is important that this lineage be understood and acknowledged because that is what establishes the truth in our stories of Tatanka Iyotake.

My goal is to enlighten all people about the real Sitting Bull. It has been difficult to attempt this delicate journey of putting the oral stories told to me by my mother into a written biography because these stories of our great-grandfather's history are in Lakota, and it is not easy to translate these words into the American written language. I wrote this book in the third person, in the same fashion as the oral history was told to me. I use the name Tatanka Iyotake to identify my great-grandfather because that was his name, Buffalo Bull Who Sits Down. I feel the name given to him by the white Americans did not truly identify the real Tatanka Iyotake. Sitting Bull does not mean Buffalo Bull Who Sits Down.

There have been many stories written about our great-grandfather and movies made about him and his life, but the irony of it all is that none of it is particularly accurate. The first person to write anything about our great-grandfather was a man named Walter Campbell, who used the pen name of Stanley Vestal. He came to the Standing Rock Indian Reservation in the late 1920s and early 1930s because it was assumed, then as well as now, that all of Sitting Bull's relatives lived there. This was not and is not true. He interviewed the betrayers and murderers of our great-grandfather. Sitting Bull's nephew, One Bull, and One Bull's daughter, Cecilia, were the main sources of information along with Bull Head and Eugene Little Soldier—not to be confused with Sitting Bull's stepson, Henry Little Soldier. It seems that Cecilia was the one who described her father as being Sitting Bull's adopted son. Tatanka Iyotake never adopted One Bull because Lakota do not adopt blood relatives. An adoption is a choice, and both sides have to agree on taking the other as a relative. If you are already related, this cannot happen. Vestal wrote a book based on these interviews titled *Sitting Bull, Champion of the Sioux.*

The only writer who made an attempt to interview the blood relatives at the Pine Ridge Reservation was Walter Camp, but he died before he was able to publish his book about the Indian Wars. Walter Camp also visited Sitting Bull's nephew, White Bull, on the Cheyenne River Reservation and learned about Sitting Bull's daughter, Standing Holy, who was the only living child in 1912. Why Vestal never came to Pine Ridge to talk to Standing Holy or her half-brothers, John Sitting Bull (Refuses Them) and Henry Little Soldier, is not known. Maybe he was not told about them, or maybe he chose to ignore them.

Stanley Vestal's work and his archived interviews have become the basis for many other books, some more scholarly than others. Historians, scholars, and authors treat Vestal's work as true and accurate, and very few have sought to investigate what the descendants know about Tatanka Iyotake. My mother was afraid to tell the story because many times when she mentioned her relationship to Tatanka Iyotake, the daughters of One Bull came to threaten her. At one time my mother was attacked by one of One Bull's daughters in the streets

17
◇

of Rapid City, South Dakota. As a young boy of about five years old, I was shocked to see how violently these women behaved. I am ready to tell the story now because the story needs to be told.

I think it is time that we natives tell our own stories. Our culture and our history have to be told by us. We lived it, and continue to live it, and I think the anthropologists and white authors have run blindly through our ancestors' legacy and our culture for far too long.

Ho Hetchetu Yelo, Pilamaya Pelo,
ERNIE LaPOINTE

18
◇

INTRODUCTION

*"Great men are usually destroyed
by those who are jealous of them."*

TATANKA IYOTAKE

At daybreak on December 15, 1890, Tatanka Iyotake's settlement was quiet and unguarded. Forty-three Metal Breasts—the Indian police force appointed by the Indian agent James McLaughlin— moved quietly into the camp, intent on arresting or eliminating the agent's rival for leadership of the Hunkpapa Lakota. A detachment of cavalry waited a short distance away to provide support.

There was only one problem: Tatanka Iyotake had two wives and two cabins. The police had to search both houses before they found the old leader asleep in the larger cabin.

By the time Tatanka Iyotake had dressed, the camp was roused. His followers gathered outside the cabin. Police cleared a path through the crowd, and Lieutenant Bull Head and Sergeant Shave Head escorted Tatanka Iyotake toward the horses. Sergeant Red Tomahawk walked at Tatanka Iyotake's back with a revolver at the chief's head.

Intent on preventing the arrest, Tatanka Iyotake's followers began to press in on the police, and a struggle erupted. Catch the Bear, one of Tatanka Iyotake's people, fired and hit Bull Head in the side. As Bull Head fell, he shot Tatanka Iyotake through the chest. Red Tomahawk also shot Tatanka Iyotake, once through the heart and then in the head.

Fourteen people died that day. These included Tatanka Iyotake, his son Crowfoot, his Assiniboine little brother Jumping Bull, and five of his followers.

On that fateful morning, the life of a father, grandfather, leader, holy man, and Sun Dancer ended near the Grand River on the Standing Rock Indian Reservation. The moment the spirit left Tatanka Iyotake's body, the spiritual untying of his relatives and *tiyospaye* (extended family) occurred, and it has continued that way for nearly 120 years.

JUMPING
BADGER

The life of this Lakota Sun Dancer began back in 1831. This is when the Bad Bow band of the Hunkpapa tribe of the Tiatunwa Lakota Nation was camped on the banks of the Elk River, now known as the Yellowstone River, in Montana. Tiatunwa means "Looking for a Homesite." These people traveled over vast areas, pursuing the buffalo and roaming freely through immense open territories. The whites mispronounced their name and called them "Teton."

The child was the second of four children born to Her Holy Door Woman and Returns Again, and was to be their only son. His older sister was Good Feather Woman, while his younger twin sisters were called Twin Woman and Brown Shawl Woman.

Returns Again was very proud of his newborn son and gave the infant his childhood name, Jumping Badger. In the Lakota culture, the young boy received his first name from something his father had seen or experienced. His adult name was given to acknowledge a noteworthy deed he accomplished in his adolescence or adulthood.

Jumping Badger was different from the other boys his age. Where the others were adventurous, eager, and often reckless, Jumping Badger always held back, thinking before he leaped. If he had lived in this century, he would have been considered a gifted child and would have been praised for his self-discipline and for always analyzing everything before he acted.

His own people, though, misunderstood, thinking his behavior was hesitant and feeble. They gave him a nickname. They started calling him Hunkesni, "slow-moving," "weak."

In the Lakota culture, when a boy reached a certain age his father would approach either a brother or a brother-in-law. He would give this trusted man a gift and a filled pipe. Then the father would ask for his help in sharing with his son the Lakota way of being. Through example and stories, the uncle would show the boy how to be a man, a warrior, and a provider for his family. For a Lakota boy, while his father was a familiar figure for whom he might feel great affection, his uncle was an authority, a person to be respected and admired. A boy would listen to his uncle.

Returns Again approached his brother Four Horns for his assistance. Four Horns was the chief of the Bad Bow band of the Hunkpapa tribe, a man with deep wisdom and many honors. Jumping Badger was fortunate to have this uncle as his mentor.

Four Horns was also a medicine man, and through his spiritual advisors he knew his young nephew was a special and gifted boy. The boy's endless curiosity and analytical abilities meant that his uncle would not have to discipline him; Jumping Badger would be ready to listen to his father's brother's wisdom. Four Horns was honored to be asked and was delighted to share in the upbringing of Jumping Badger.

In agreeing to teach Jumping Badger, Four Horns also agreed to take the boy into his own household. For the rest of his childhood, Jumping Badger would live with his uncle, following him and learning from him all the knowledge he would need to be a good Lakota man.

When Jumping Badger was about seven years old, he had already made a bow with some arrows. With patience and a lot of hard work, he managed to fashion one perfect arrow, getting it balanced and true. This was a real accomplishment for a seven-year-old, and the boy was pleased and proud of his good arrow.

In the Bad Bow band there was one man who was a gifted bow and arrow maker. One day he set a test for all the young boys of the band who were between the ages of six and ten years old. He asked them to go hunting and bring him a beautiful bird. He told the boys that he would give a fine bow and arrows with a quiver to the first one who brought him such a bird.

The boys went in different directions, hunting earnestly for the most beautiful bird in the whole area. Jumping Badger hunted too, rejecting bird after bird as being not beautiful enough. Finally he spotted a Bullock's oriole sitting at the top of a tree. At last, he thought, a truly beautiful bird! He took careful aim.

Another young boy, coming from a different direction, saw the same bird. As Jumping Badger analyzed the situation, this boy immediately shot an arrow at the oriole. He missed, and his arrow got tangled in the branches near the top of the tree. The boy was disappointed about missing the bird and very sad about losing his best arrow.

Jumping Badger, who hadn't even got his chance to shoot at the bird, still volunteered to help by trying to shoot the boy's arrow out of the tree. He was successful in knocking the arrow down, but when it fell to the ground, it broke. The boy instantly changed from sad to angry. He accused Jumping Badger of breaking his good arrow and was ready to fight.

Jumping Badger analyzed the new situation and offered the boy his own perfect arrow. Though he had spent time getting his arrow balanced and true, he was willing to sacrifice it to avoid a pointless fight.

None of the boys shot a beautiful bird that day, but when they returned to camp they all talked about the incident between Jumping Badger and the other boy, telling how a fight was avoided. The arrow maker was impressed by how Jumping Badger successfully avoided a fight and kept the peace. As a reward for this wise behavior, he gave Jumping Badger the fine set of bow and arrows with a quiver.

He was still called Hunkesni by the people, but he was steadily gaining their respect. Like all Lakota boys, he acquired the skill of riding horses. He practiced until he was also a great shot with the bow and arrows. He learned how to track and stalk game really well. Through practice, games, and competition, the boy was gaining all the knowledge and abilities he would need as a Lakota man.

When Jumping Badger was ten years old, Four Horns decided it was time to test his nephew's tracking and hunting skills. The camp had moved closer to a big buffalo herd. While the rest of the hunters made preparations to go after the big herd, Four Horns took his nephew and told him to track a smaller herd farther to the west.

His skills at tracking and stalking were excellent for one so young, and his uncle was pleased when Jumping Badger found the smaller herd. Though there were only 100 to 150 head of buffalo in this herd, buffalo are dangerous animals to hunt. Stampeding buffalo can easily run down a horse and trample its rider into the dust. Four Horns advised Jumping Badger to be very careful, as this was his first hunt, and not to get caught in the center of the herd.

Jumping Badger proceeded to ride right into the middle of the herd with his arrow fitted into the bow. He went after a big buffalo bull. His shot was true and he felled the big bull. The rest of the herd spooked and ran away, fortunately not trampling Jumping Badger in their panic.

Four Horns was angry but also proud of his nephew. He asked Jumping Badger why he chose this particular big bull when there was a cow closer to the edge of the herd he could have taken. The boy replied that he had seen the cow, but he also saw her calf. If he had taken the cow, her calf would surely have perished as well.

The compassion of his young nephew amazed Four Horns. He instructed Jumping Badger to eat a portion of the liver of the buffalo. The liver, which filters toxins from the body, is the most polluted part of the animal. Eating the liver was a way to thank the Spirit of the buffalo for giving his life so the people could survive. Then Four Horns told the young boy to get his mother and relatives to help in preparing the meat.

Jumping Badger rode fast to his mother's tipi and asked her to bring her sharp knives and all the relatives for the preparing of the meat. As she collected her skinning and butchering tools, Jumping Badger gave his mother yet another reason to be proud of him. He took her outside and quietly indicated a nearby tipi where a widow lived with her two children. He told his mother to cut some of the choice portions of the meat and give them to the widow. Since she had no one to provide for herself and her children, this was his way of contributing to their welfare. Jumping Badger had just exhibited his compassion and generosity, and he was only ten years old.

Earning
His Name

eturns Again, Jumping Badger's father, was a deeply spiritual man and had the ability to communicate with the four-legged. One time, around the time Jumping Badger killed his first buffalo, Returns Again was part of a scouting group looking for buffalo. The group had camped for the night when a big white buffalo bull suddenly appeared at the edge of the campfire. The scouting party was startled and they scattered—except for Returns Again. The buffalo bull reared up on his haunches and bellowed as he stomped down on his fore hooves. He did this four times and then turned and disappeared into the night.

The rest of the scouts returned to the fire, wondering about the reason the buffalo did this. Returns Again said the bull had come to give him a gift. The gift was four names the buffalo had bellowed. The first name was Tatanka Iyotake, the second was Tatanka Psica, the third was Tatanka Wajila, and the fourth was Tatanka Wi Uha Naji. The names were Buffalo Bull Sits Down (Sitting Bull), Jumping Bull, One Bull, and Bull Stands with Cow. Returns Again told his friends this was a special blessing and gift from the buffalo nation, and he took the first name for himself. He said, "From this day forward I will be known as Tatanka Iyotake."

. . .

Jumping Badger had learned many things through stories and by observing the examples of his uncle Four Horns. He learned the creation stories and how the Lakota people received the gift of the Sacred Pipe and the ceremonies that came with it. Four Horns explained to Jumping Badger that he must be brave and compassionate and show fortitude, and he must always seek wisdom from Wakan Tanka, the Great Spirit. A true warrior knows more than how to bring food to his family or kill an enemy. In fact, it was considered much more courageous not to kill the enemy but to count coup instead by touching the body of the enemy warrior with a special coup stick without physically harming him. The warrior who could perform a "bloodless coup" was entitled to high praise. The enemy who had coup counted on him was greatly shamed.

When Jumping Badger was fourteen years old, he joined a raiding party along with his uncle, Four Horns, and his father, Tatanka Iyotake. A band of Crows had camped in a valley with their many fine horses. The temptation was irresistible to the Lakota, who sneaked up as close as they could, then charged into the camp, surprising the Crows.

Jumping Badger was one of the first to reach the startled Crow warriors. He counted coup on one of the Crow warriors with the coup stick Four Horns had given him. The other Lakota warriors were all witnesses to Jumping Badger's successful coup. Jumping Badger's father was so proud of his son, he came and embraced him and said,

"Today you are a warrior. You are now a man."

The raiding party was successful in acquiring many fine horses, but on this day, the celebration began when the warriors returned to the camp. Tatanka Iyotake offered a great feast. There was dancing and eating and telling of heroic deeds of the past. Finally, Tatanka Iyotake asked for silence and told the people, "Today we celebrate the birth of a warrior."

He told of Jumping Badger's first coup and how his bravery had manifested itself. When Tatanka Iyotake finished telling of Jumping Badger's brave deed, he asked some warriors to bring horses into the center of the camp. In recognition of his son's bravery, Tatanka Iyotake proceeded to give away these horses. He walked around the circle, giving horses to those who needed them.

He kept one last horse, a magnificent bay. Approaching Jumping Badger, he said,

"I place this eagle tail feather in your hair as a symbol for your first coup. I give you this fine bay horse, a warrior's horse, and this shield; and may they serve you well." In appearance, the shield was round and made of hardened buffalo hide. The design featured a black thunderbird in the center. Two semicircles ringed the thunderbird, one of them red and one black. The shield was one that the boy would carry throughout his years as a Hunkpapa warrior.

Tatanka Iyotake dipped his hand into a pot, and when he withdrew it, his hand was black. He proceeded to cover his son's body with the black paint. Then he announced,

"This is my son; and on this day he is no longer naked, for he is a warrior of the Bad Bow band of the Hunkpapa Lakota Nation. From this day forward, I shall be Jumping Bull and this warrior's name shall be Tatanka Iyotake." In this way the father of Jumping Badger conferred on his son the adult name he would bear for the rest of his life. At that moment, "Jumping Badger" ceased to exist, and Tatanka Iyotake began his distinguished life.

The battle record of the Lakota was unmatched by any other Plains tribes, so the expectations of a Hunkpapa warrior were high. Tatanka Iyotake was steadily gaining respect and prestige, and he was never an unwilling participant in battle.

He was fifteen years old when a band of Flatheads ambushed the Lakota warriors. The Flatheads were well entrenched and were raining down arrows and bullets on the Lakota. Tatanka Iyotake told the other warriors he was going to run the daring line. Running the daring line meant riding between the two opposing forces within the range of the enemies' weapons. The rider became a moving target for the combined forces of the enemy warriors. There was a high risk of injury or death to the warrior who rode the daring line.

Tatanka Iyotake increased the level of risk by sitting upright on his horse as he ran the line, instead of using his horse's neck for cover. He faced a hail of bullets and arrows, but none found their mark until he reached the end of the line. Then a musket ball struck his left foot. Although the wound was painful, he did not retreat from the battle.

Later, when the warriors returned to camp, another celebration was held for Tatanka Iyotake. He was recognized for his battlefield wound and was given a red eagle feather. He counted coup 69 times during the coming years and was wounded in battle at least three times. He was entitled to wear an eagle feather for each of these accomplishments. Tatanka Iyotake, however, was a humble man. He chose to identify himself simply, wearing just one eagle feather straight up, representing his first coup against the Crow, and the single red feather, symbolizing his first battle wound, slightly slanted to the right.

THE STRONG HEART SOCIETY

As young men became recognized as warriors, they were chosen by the various men's societies to become new members. These groups of men consisted of all the adult males responsible for protecting and providing for the people. While the white culture has called these "warrior societies," in fact they were much more than that. Each group of men shared a sense of identity and a larger responsibility toward the whole group that went far beyond a purely military definition. A man had to prove his worth to be invited to join such a society. Once he was a member, his ongoing behavior reflected back on all the others. This meant that members of the societies were bound to uphold the honor of the group in war and in peace.

Tatanka Iyotake was invited to become a member of the Strong Heart Society. The Strong Heart Society was the most prestigious of the warrior societies within the Hunkpapa Nation, consisting of around fifty of the bravest and most compassionate warriors of the Hunkpapa tribe. Not only were they the protectors of the people, but they were also providers and caretakers for the needy and orphans.

Within the Strong Heart Society there were two warriors chosen to be sash bearers. These two warriors pledged to ride into battle and stake their sashes to the ground and fight until victory or death. They remained staked to the ground until another member of the society released them. Tatanka Iyotake became one of the sash bearers at the age of seventeen.

The Strong Heart Society warriors had been looking for a Crow camp. They were planning on taking horses, and when some scouts came back to report a Crow camp not far from where they were, they decided to surprise them under cover of darkness. The Lakota were successful and took many horses; but the Crow were in pursuit, so the Lakota warriors decided to stop and face the enemy.

The Crows did not expect to find the Hunkpapa waiting for them as they came over a rise. Even though they were surprised, three of the Crow warriors charged daringly into the Hunkpapa ranks. One of the Crow counted coup on two Lakota, while the second Crow warrior fired his rifle and killed a Lakota warrior. A Hunkpapa warrior rode out to challenge the third Crow. This Lakota warrior dismounted his horse and shouted, "I am Tatanka Iyotake, and I have come to fight!"

Tatanka Iyotake's reputation as a great warrior had not spread across the land yet, but the Crow warrior would have noticed this Lakota warrior's attire. He wore a regal headdress which featured blackened buffalo horns with the hair still attached. He had a red woolen sash adorned with eagle feathers draped over his shoulder. The Crows had heard of such warriors and of their bravery. The Crow warrior knew he was facing a sash bearer from the Strong Heart Society.

Just the knowledge of who he faced would be chilling, but the Crow warriors were also brave. The challenged Crow warrior dismounted his horse and started running toward the Strong Heart warrior. Now the Lakota warrior had a chance to observe his Crow opponent. His style of regalia identified him as a chief.

The Crow chief was carrying a flintlock rifle and the distance between the two warriors was closing fast. The Crow suddenly dropped to one knee and raised his rifle. Tatanka Iyotake dropped to the ground and took shelter behind his shield. The Crow fired and his ball hit the shield. It ricocheted and struck Tatanka Iyotake in the left foot.

Tatanka Iyotake dropped his shield, took aim, and shot the Crow in the chest. Then he limped over to the Crow chief and slipped his knife into the Crow's heart. The powers associated with the chief were, through this act, transferred to the victor. The rest of the Lakota warriors then attacked the other Crow and scattered them into a full retreat.

This second wound to his left foot did not heal properly, and for the rest of his life Tatanka Iyotake walked with a limp. The limp did not hamper his abilities, as he could still run fast, but it served as a constant reminder to others of his bravery and courage.

By the time he was in his midtwenties, Tatanka Iyotake had been elected to be a leader of the Strong Heart Society. He formed within the Strong Heart Society a sub-group consisting of an alliance of volunteer warriors that held their meetings and council at midnight. This alliance was the Midnight Strong Heart Society. It was most uncommon to choose someone so young to hold a leadership position, but Tatanka Iyotake elevated the position to greater heights and did not disappoint those who chose him.

33
◇

JUMPING BULL

In the late 1850s, an important event occurred in the family life
of Tatanka Iyotake. The Strong Heart Society, traveling north of
the Missouri River, encountered an Assiniboine camp. It was a
single family camped on the riverbank, and the Strong Heart warriors
surprised the family members. The family attempted to defend its
camp but was no match for the warriors, who wiped out the whole
family—except for one young boy. He was about eleven years old, still
with only a child's bow and arrows. Even so, he kept attempting to
shoot at the warriors. The warriors decided to wait for Tatanka Iyotake
to arrive and let him decide the fate of this bold and desperate child.

When Tatanka Iyotake arrived and dismounted his horse, the
young Hohe (Assiniboine) seized his only chance to survive. He ran to
the Strong Heart leader, embraced him around the waist, and pleaded
with him, saying, "Big brother, save me!"

Though the boy could not have known it, he spoke directly to the
heart of Tatanka Iyotake. He just finished mourning the death of his
firstborn son. In addition, he himself was an only son; he did not have

any younger brothers. Tatanka Iyotake told the warriors he wanted to spare the boy's life and that he wished to take him as his brother.

Tatanka Iyotake's request to make the little Assiniboine his brother was brought in front of the elders, since it would require a Hunkayapi ceremony. The Hunkayapi is one of the ceremonies associated with the gift of the Sacred Pipe. It allows Lakota men and women to create relationships with people not related to them by blood. The purpose of the Hunkayapi is for the Lakota to make relatives among warring tribes to eliminate wars and create peace among the Nations. Because of this, it is a serious undertaking. Those who have a Hunka relationship have deliberately chosen to be responsible for each other. Their ties are deeper and even more important than the relationship between blood kin. The elders examined and debated the issue to make sure both Tatanka Iyotake and the young Assiniboine desired the Hunka.

The two then went through a Hunkayapi ceremony that confirmed their choice of each other as relatives. Once that ceremony was completed, they were bound together for life. They were pledged to protect and care for each other to the death. This solemn bond was honored by both men throughout their lives. Because the boy refused to return to his own people, Tatanka Iyotake called his Hunka brother Stays Back; but others called him Little Assiniboine.

The summer after this Hunkayapi ceremony, a party of Strong Heart Society warriors was scouting for buffalo. Tatanka Iyotake was part of this group, along with his little brother, Stays Back, and his aging father, Jumping Bull.

While some members of the group scouted, others were busy looking for a new campsite. Tatanka Iyotake and Stays Back were with the scouting party, but Jumping Bull had stayed in camp, suffering from a toothache. As he grew more elderly, he had many aches and pains, but the toothache was the worst of all. It only worsened with time. Still, he worked with the other elders and the women of the group to set up their tipis.

Unknown to them, a band of Crow warriors was watching from cover as the Hunkpapa were making camp. The Crow sprang their ambush on the unsuspecting Lakota. Two Lakota warriors were taken down by arrows, but the Strong Hearts recovered quickly and repelled the attack.

One Crow warrior remained behind, and Jumping Bull said, "He is mine."

Forgetting the aches and pains of age, even the awful toothache that had been plaguing him, he raced in front of everyone else and took aim with his bow and arrow. The Crow, however, jumped off his horse and fired his rifle, hitting Jumping Bull in the shoulder and knocking him off balance.

Jumping Bull regained his balance and resumed his charge. The Crow reached for his knife, as did Jumping Bull, but in the end his age betrayed him. He was not as fast or as nimble as the Crow. The Crow plunged his knife into Jumping Bull's chest, pulled it out, and struck him on the top of the head. Jumping Bull fell dead.

Tatanka Iyotake returned shortly after the fight and was told of his father's death. Jumping Bull had died just before his son returned. Tatanka Iyotake set out in pursuit of the Crow, and when he caught up to them, he killed the warrior who had taken Jumping Bull's life. The rest of the Lakota warriors, though outnumbered, fought the remaining Crow until just a few escaped.

Two Crow women were captured and brought back to the Lakota camp. The future looked grim for these two, since the Lakota people wanted to avenge Jumping Bull's death. When the warriors saw the mourning Tatanka Iyotake, his clothes torn, his braids cut off, and tears running down his face, they were even more determined to execute the Crow women.

Even in the midst of his grieving, Tatanka Iyotake showed his wisdom and compassion. He told the people not to harm the women. He said his father had been a warrior and this was a warrior's death.

The people mourned for four days and then held a celebration of the victory over the Crow. Tatanka Iyotake joined in the festivities as the new head of his family. When the end of summer approached, the people gave the two Crow women gifts and horses, and allowed them to return to their people.

After four days of mourning, Tatanka Iyotake's father, Jumping Bull, was buried. Now it was time for Tatanka Iyotake to perform the first ceremony that was given to the people with the sacred pipe. The ceremony was the "Keeping of the Soul." This practice is the way for the relatives to keep the soul (spirit) of a person that has died. The purpose is to keep the memory and spirit with the family for one year.

A lock of hair is cut from the deceased and kept with the family in their tipi. During the time period of the "keeping of the soul," the family integrates the spirit of the deceased into their daily life. The spirit is treated with courtesy. Food and water are offered as if the spirit were a living member of the family.

When the one-year anniversary has come, then the "Releasing of the Soul" ceremony is performed. Now the relatives invite the camp or village to attend a feast and a giveaway. They give away all the deceased person's belongings to the less fortunate in the camp. They also formally release the soul or spirit to make the journey to the Spirit World. The lock of hair is either buried or burned, and *wakapa pi* (pounded dried buffalo meat) is offered for the spirit's journey.

There is no word for goodbye in the Lakota language. Instead, when Lakota part from one another they say "*Toksha Ake*," which means "See you again." The "Releasing of the Soul" ceremony is just a temporary parting until the relatives are reunited in the spirit world.

It was during this time that Tatanka Iyotake felt the memory of his father would be best carried on by bestowing his sacred name on one who would carry the name with humility, respect, and admiration for his father. At the conclusion of the "Releasing of the Soul" ceremony, he called for a naming ceremony to bestow the name Jumping Bull on a person worthy to walk with this name in honor and respect.

He chose his Hunka brother Stays Back, or as others called him, Little Assiniboine. Leading his Hunka brother to the center of the camp, Tatanka Iyotake told the people his decision to give his father's sacred name to Stays Back. He tied an eagle plume on Stays Back's hair and told the people, "From this day forward his name shall be Jumping Bull."

Then he had another giveaway. His Hunka brother was mounted on a fine horse and led around the camp singing songs of praise for his new name. The new Jumping Bull was very respectful of the name and carried it with honor until his death on December 15, 1890.

WIVES AND CHILDREN

The Lakota understand that there are four difficult things in life. The first is to lose your firstborn, the second is to lose your wife, the third is not to have enough food for your family, and the fourth is to encounter a larger group of enemy warriors. Tatanka Iyotake would experience all four of these hardships during his lifetime.

Tatanka Iyotake showed a maturity and understanding of life that far exceeded other young men his age. His level of responsibility was also much higher. He was required to care for his people at many levels. His position also required him to make wise decisions on behalf of the group, and he was responsible for their overall well-being. Tatanka Iyotake needed the help of a wife to fulfill all the duties of caring for the people. As a result, he married while he was still in his twenties. This was unusual for Lakota men of that time, since they did not consider marriage until a man was in his thirties or even his forties. The woman he chose to become his wife was Light Hair.

Living arrangements for married couples among the Lakota were based on the fact that a woman owned the tipi. Women were in charge of the shelter of their families and everything that went with that. Only if a woman asked a man for help could he take part in these tasks, and then he was limited to a few things, like helping put up the tipi or helping with such household chores as gathering wood or hauling water. When Tatanka Iyotake and Light Hair married, she owned their home, and she would be completely in charge of it.

It was not long before Light Hair became pregnant. In 1857, less than two years after they had married, she bore Tatanka Iyotake his first child, a son.

In those days, childbearing was the most dangerous thing a woman could do. Any kind of complication could lead to the death of the mother, the child, or both of them. Light Hair was only twenty-four years old, but she did not survive the birth of her son. Tatanka Iyotake mourned the loss of his young wife, but he was proud of the son she bore him.

When a man with young children lost his wife, his immediate family members, his sisters and/or mother would be there to help in caring for him and his children. If he did not have a mother or sister, the help would come from his extended family, such as female cousins, or, if he had married brothers, from his brothers' wives.

The widower and his children would continue to live in the tipi he had shared with his deceased wife. His female relatives would care for the tipi and do the basic chores, such as cooking and helping in raising the small children.

In the time of Tatanka Iyotake, the Lakota people did not ignore the children. Sometimes the whole village would care for them. Children were considered as "something sacred is growing," and they were provided with the best care possible. Sometimes, though, sickness would win and take the small children. This was the case with Tatanka Iyotake's son. He was stricken with an illness and made the journey to the Spirit World at the young age of four years old. Deeply saddened, Tatanka Iyotake was again in mourning. Within four years he had experienced two of the worst difficulties of a Lakota man's life.

After the death of his father, Jumping Bull, in 1859, Tatanka Iyotake assumed the responsibility of taking care of his mother, Her Holy Door. He kept his tipi next to hers so he could provide her with security and protection.

When Tatanka Iyotake married again, he chose a woman named Snow On Her. She bore him two daughters: Many Horses, born in 1865, and Walks Looking, born in 1868. Tatanka Iyotake, a man who loved children, was very fond of his daughters. In 1866, he decided to take a second wife. He chose to marry Red Woman. It was one of the few times in his life that Tatanka Iyotake made a mistake in judgment.

The two women did not get along. Usually, when a man chose multiple wives, they were sisters so they could work together in harmony. The first wife, usually older, was senior and usually held a slightly higher position. Because Tatanka Iyotake loved and cared for his two wives equally, he expected the two women to also respect and care for each other equally.

Snow On Her, however, was not happy to have the assistance Red Woman could provide. Instead, she was extremely jealous of the new wife, especially since the two of them were the same age, reducing her natural authority over the other woman. Furthermore, Tatanka Iyotake seemed to show a marked preference for Red Woman's company. Snow On Her became bitter and hostile. She caused great disturbances in the camp with her anger toward Red Woman. Her displays of emotion were most unseemly and shocking to everybody within the village.

Instead of promoting her husband's position within the tribe and providing an example of a harmonious household, Snow On Her caused considerable social disapproval. Tatanka Iyotake, for all his peacemaking skills, was not able to curb this bad behavior by his wife. To make matters worse, he really did prefer Red Woman.

Eventually, tiring of the controversy, Tatanka Iyotake took the drastic step of divorcing Snow On Her. He sent her back to her family, and the disruptions to daily life ceased. The two daughters she had born Tatanka Iyotake, however, remained with their father. Many Horses and Walks Looking would grow up in their father's household with their paternal grandmother and their father's other wives and children.

In 1870, Red Woman bore a son. By 1871, she, too, was dead. This child would now become the responsibility of Tatanka Iyotake's mother and extended family.

By this time, Tatanka Iyotake was forty years old, widowed twice and divorced once, and had three small children. His responsibilities continued to increase, and he still needed a wife. Roughly a year after the death of Red Woman, he married again. This time he chose a widow, Seen By Her Nation. Shortly thereafter, he also married her widowed sister, Four Robes. The two women had lived with their brother, Grey Eagle. Each one of them brought a son into the new marriage. Seen By Her Nation's son was Refuses Them, a deaf mute, who would later be known as John Sitting Bull. Four Robes' son was Little Soldier; he was known as Henry Little Soldier.

At last, the domestic life of Tatanka Iyotake stabilized. These sisters worked together in harmony for the remainder of Tatanka Iyotake's life. Seen By Her Nation was the mother of Crowfoot and Standing Holy Woman. Four Robes bore Lodge In Sight Woman and two sets of twin boys. Only one of the four boys survived—Runs Away From, later known as William Sitting Bull. Four Robes also gave birth to another girl, who died before she reached her first birthday. In addition, the two women took responsibility for the other three children: Many Horses, Walks Looking, and the unnamed son of Red Woman.

43

◆

GAZING AT THE SUN: THE FIRST VISION

Four Horns showed many things by example, including how to make a pipe and stem. This is a requirement for individuals seeking to pray and perform ceremonies. He made sure Tatanka Iyotake learned and understood the powerful significance of the Wiwang Wacipi (Gazing at the Sun as You Dance), abbreviated by white culture to Sun Dance. Tatanka Iyotake made a commitment to perform the Wiwang Wacipi. To do this, he first performed the Inipi, the sweat lodge ceremony used to purify the soul. Then he undertook the Hanblecheyapi (Crying for a Vision through the Night) or vision quest, seeking guidance from the spirits.

The Wiwang Wacipi is a ceremony an individual performs for the health and welfare of the people. It is also a fertility ceremony for the continued existence of the Nation. The pledger dances while staring at the sun and offering prayers through the eagle bone whistle.

Preparation for the sacred ceremony begins with choosing an open area and creating a circle sixty feet in diameter. The center of the circle is where the Wiwang Wacipi pole is placed. A Wicasa Wakan (holy man) will select a cottonwood tree, which will become the Wiwang Wacipi pole, and mark it for the ceremony.

The evening before the Wiwang Wacipi, the warriors from the camp track and find the marked tree. They attack the tree as an enemy and begin counting coup on it.

Once the enemy tree has been defeated, a pure young woman steps forward to make the first four cuts on the tree, one for each cardinal direction. It is a high honor for a maiden to perform this task, since the girl represents the White Buffalo Calf Woman.

Cutting down the Wiwang Wacipi pole is an honor granted to the pledgers of the Wiwang Wacipi. The tree cannot touch the ground and those at the cutting ceremony will carry the cottonwood to the Wiwang Wacipi area and place it on a bed made of large branches. Offerings and spiritual symbols are tied to its branches and trunk before the tree is raised. A bough of chokecherry branches will be placed in the fork of the tree. Attached to one end of the chokecherry bough is a small figure of a Wiwang Wacipi man with an erect penis. On the other end is a small buffalo figure, also with an erect penis. These figures represent fertility, a prayer that the Lakota nation and the buffalo nation will always be populous and fruitful.

In the center of the sixty-foot circular area, a hole is dug and wakapa pi (pounded meat), tobacco, and chokecherry juice offerings are put in the hole as gifts to the tree, which is then raised into position by leather ropes. Sharp-edged gravel is thrown inside the area to create more suffering for the barefooted dancers. The arena is now ready.

A man who commits to the Wiwang Wacipi offers to give his sweat

45
◈

and spill his blood for the well-being and continued existence of his people. Before he begins the ceremony, he will purify himself through Inipi ceremonies. Only when his body, mind, and spirit are purified will he continue.

The pledger commits to extensive suffering for his people and allows his upper body flesh to be pierced by sharpened bones or sticks. The piercing bones are attached to leather ropes that are connected to buffalo skulls that the pledger will drag around the circular arena, or they may be attached to the Wiwang Wacipi pole that is in the center of the grounds. In either case, the dancer gazes into the sun, blowing on an eagle bone whistle, and pulls against the piercing bones until they tear free from his skin.

Tatanka Iyotake committed to be pierced on his back and chest and to be suspended above the ground, hanging by the skewers that impaled him. The pain was tremendous and he went into a shock-induced trance state. In this trance, he envisioned himself as a young boy, resting by a tree.

As he lay there in his trance, he heard a voice telling him to be absolutely still. Then he felt the coarse hair and smelled the rancid breath of a huge grizzly bear. In his vision, Tatanka Iyotake lay motionless. The bear finally left because bears usually do not have any interest in things they think are already dead.

The boy looked up to see who had warned him to lie still. Sitting on the branches above his head was a woodpecker. Tatanka Iyotake thanked the woodpecker and told him that from this day forward the Zintkala Oyate (bird nation) would be his relatives.

The next instant he was transformed into a young man walking through the woods. He came upon a wolf with two arrows in his side.

The injured wolf said, "Boy, if you help me, all the nations will know your name."

Tatanka Iyotake removed the arrows and, as the wolf limped away, Tatanka Iyotake found himself in another place, this time as an adult. He was seated next to a Wicasa Wakan. The Wicasa Wakan sat silently as Tatanka Iyotake told him of his vision. Then he said, "You have experienced much. You have seen the buffalo, the Thunder Beings have visited you, and you are blessed by Wakan Tanka." He painted the young man's face with streaks of lightning, giving him his sacred colors and design. These are given to young men for the protection of their soul/spirit. Whenever Tatanka Iyotake left the camp, he always painted his forehead yellow with a red lightning bolt running straight down his face from above his eyebrow to his jaw.

When he had finished, the Wicasa Wakan said, "Your honor is great, but your responsibilities are greater."

The words of the Wicasa Wakan were still echoing in his head when the piercing bones ripped through Tatanka Iyotake's flesh and he fell to the ground. Tatanka Iyotake had finished his first Wiwang Wacipi. His visions during the ceremony confirmed that he was now a holy man as his father and uncle had been. He could now communicate with Wakan Tanka and all his creations.

Encountering the Americans

The Hunkpapa had not engaged the Wasicu (white Americans) in warfare yet, but they were now starting to encroach on the hunting grounds of the Hunkpapa. By this time, the Nations knew the reputation of the Wasicu—once they arrived, they did not leave willingly; whatever they took, they never gave back; and they did not share. The Hunkpapa resigned themselves to the knowledge that war was inevitable.

In 1863, General Alfred Sully requested a meeting with the Hunkpapa to discuss a peace treaty. Tatanka Iyotake trusted Sully no more than he did any other Wasicu. Trust had to be earned, and so far, the Wasicu had not attempted to earn it. Furthermore, the peace treaties they made with other Nations were always broken. Not even one had been honored. Tatanka Iyotake declined Sully's invitation to meet.

The following year, the two leaders did meet when Sully attacked Tatanka Iyotake's camp at Killdeer Mountain. This encounter came about because of events that took place two years earlier and hundreds of miles to the east, in Minnesota. The Dakota uprising was a rebellion by the eastern relatives of the Tiatunwa Lakota. Brief but bloody, this rebellion resulted in the hanging deaths of thirty-eight of the Dakota involved. Some of the Dakota fled north into Canada; some went westward; and some joined Tatanka Iyotake's people.

Sully pursued these fugitives. When he found them at Killdeer Mountain, he attacked the greatly outnumbered Lakota, leaving one hundred Lakota dead. Tatanka Iyotake came to some quick and sobering realizations about the way the Wasicu soldiers—the Long Knives—fought. They fought to kill without any honor or personal glory. Tatanka Iyotake did not enjoy fighting on these terms, but he had very few options.

At the same time, though, he learned the weaknesses of the way in which the Long Knives fought. They always stayed together in a group. Lakota warriors fought as individuals, always moving and presenting highly mobile and evasive targets. The Long Knives way of fighting meant that even a warrior with bad aim had a good chance of hitting somebody if he fired into the massed forces arrayed against him. Tatanka Iyotake took note of this.

If it had been possible, Tatanka Iyotake might have accepted peace terms that simply allowed him and his people to continue to live their traditional lifestyle. Achieving this kind of agreement, however, was highly unlikely. It would require that the Wasicu leave unsettled the vast tracts of open land the Lakota claimed as hunting territory. White settlers seemed incapable of doing this. As a result, Tatanka Iyotake adopted a policy of avoidance, refraining from attacking white settlers as long as they, in turn, left the Lakota and their hunting grounds alone.

49
◈

THE LEADER
OF THE LAKOTA

The encroachment of the white man was advancing very quickly, and this worried Four Horns. He decided that new leadership was necessary. In 1867, he sent word to all the Lakota bands and other nearby nations, requesting a gathering to discuss an important matter. There were six Lakota bands, some Yanktonai, and a few Cheyenne who responded to his call and arrived at his camp on the lower Powder River. Among those who arrived quickly were Crazy Horse and Gall. They were in agreement with Four Horns about the need for new leadership, and they understood the urgency of the situation.

Four Horns began the council by explaining to the chiefs and elders why he believed new leadership was required. He said he was advanced in age, and a younger Wicasa was desired to lead the people. He recommended his nephew, Tatanka Iyotake, to be the chief of the Tiatunwa Lakota Nation. The council members all agreed with Four Horns that Tatanka Iyotake was the best choice, for he was advanced in his thinking and actions for one who was only thirty-six years old. They also agreed to the appointment of Crazy Horse as the second chief.

This was a very significant decision. In order to underline the gravity of this action, the Lakota performed a solemn ceremony to invest Tatanka Iyotake with his new position. Four chiefs went to Tatanka Iyotake's tipi and escorted him out. They brought a buffalo robe with them and had him sit on it. Then they carried him to the council tipi for the ceremony.

Four Horns spoke. He told everyone that the council had appointed a new chief, and it was now his responsibility to see that the Tiatunwa Lakota were fed and defended. He told Tatanka Iyotake, "When you tell us to fight, we will raise up our weapons; and if you tell us to make peace, we will lay down our weapons. We will smoke the Cannupa Wakan (sacred pipe) so Wakan Tanka will bless our decision."

Tatanka Iyotake was given a magnificent bow and arrows and a rifle. He was presented with a headdress with a trailer of eagle feathers all the way down his back to the ground. Each eagle feather on the headdress represented a coup by the warrior who contributed it. Finally, he was given a magnificent white stallion. He was lifted onto its back and led around the camp. The warriors from many different societies followed behind, dressed in their finest and wearing their eagle feathers proudly.

Tatanka Iyotake was gifted in composing songs. He started to sing as he was led around the camp. He sang this song: "Oyate kihan caja mayatanpi ca blihimic'iyelo he. Tatanka Iyotake he heyakiyapilo he" ("I humble myself when my people speak my name, so said Tatanka Iyotake").

From the time of this ceremony, Tatanka Iyotake accepted the burden of responsibility for the well-being of all his people.

The Brulés under Spotted Tail and the southern Oglalas under Red Cloud did not attend the gathering. They refused to recognize Tatanka Iyotake as their chief.

ARROW CREEK

Tatanka Iyotake always kept his word by not being the aggressor against the white settlers as long as they kept the peace with his Nation. That did not mean the Lakota were at peace, only that the battles that took place were with other tribes. These skirmishes were usually over hunting rights. The fighting was traditional, with more honors granted to the warrior who counted coup than to one who killed another, but the traditions of the Wasicu were widely being adopted by the tribes across the land.

One particularly fierce battle took place in the winter of 1870 at a place called Big Dry Creek near the upper Yellowstone River. Tatanka Iyotake had three coups, but unfortunately thirty Crow warriors were killed. It was a costly fight, though, because his youngest uncle, Looks for Him in a Tent, was also killed. Once again, Tatanka Iyotake had to mourn for a close relative.

A few months later Tatanka Iyotake and a gathering of people were camped at the mouth of the Rosebud River. Calling for the attention of the people, he rose, lit his Cannupa, and told them of a vision that had come to him.

"In two days a big battle will occur and many enemies will die, as will some of the Lakota," he said. In his vision, he saw a ball of fire coming toward him; but it disappeared as it reached him.

Scouts immediately rode out. When they returned, they reported a band of Flathead camped on the buffalo hunting grounds of the Lakota. Tatanka Iyotake prepared a plan for the attack. He sent some of the younger warriors ahead to act as decoys. When the Flathead saw there were just a few, they gave chase in hopes of overwhelming the outnumbered Lakota. The young warriors fled, hotly pursued by the Flathead warriors—straight into an ambush. The main force of the Lakota warriors rose up from their hiding places to confront the startled enemy.

The battle plan worked almost to perfection. Only three Lakota died compared to the much greater losses of the Flathead. Tatanka Iyotake's prophesy was fulfilled as an arrow passed through his forearm, wounding him. The wound healed well and his reputation as a chief and Wicasa Wakan was established beyond doubt.

It was in 1872 that the Northern Pacific Railroad was planning to build a rail line through Montana Territory to Dakota Territory. The railroad sent surveyors to identify and locate the best route possible, but they were not alone. A military escort of 500 men out of Fort Ellis under the command of Major Eugene M. Baker accompanied them. The surveyors knew they were in the heart of Lakota territory but felt safe with the military escort. They established a camp near Arrow Creek.

Unknown to the surveyors, the Lakota were watching their every move. The Lakota had made camp nearby and were sitting in serious discussion about the next course of action. Suddenly, a young warrior appeared at the entrance of the tipi and interrupted the council. When Tatanka Iyotake asked what had happened, the warrior reported that the Brulés and the Hunkpapa warriors had attacked the surveyors' camp. The warriors made the decision, and the council meeting dissolved.

The Lakota warriors and the Long Knives exchanged shots all night. The Long Knives killed one Hunkpapa warrior who had run the daring line. They took his body and threw it on the campfire. The warriors were infuriated at the show of disrespect by the Long Knives.

The morning brought Tatanka Iyotake and Crazy Horse to the top of a bluff overlooking the battlefield. They realized the Long Knives were well entrenched and it would be difficult to reach them. Yet the warriors were continuing to run the daring line. There was no need for this, for they had already proven their courage.

Tatanka Iyotake soon discovered these braves were followers of a warrior who said he had had a vision. Any warrior who rode with him would be cloaked with an invisible blanket and would not be hit by arrows or bullets. His followers kept riding repeatedly between the opposing forces. Some were hit, but none was seriously injured.

Tatanka Iyotake located the warrior whose vision the young braves were following and said, "Enough; I do not want the young braves wounded or killed. Their bravery is evident and the shedding of their blood will not do us any good."

The warrior whose vision was in question spoke up and challenged in return,

"The great warrior Tatanka Iyotake perhaps has forgotten what it takes to be brave." After all, he said defiantly, "it is said that with age, blood upsets a man's stomach!"

Some of the young braves were also upset at Tatanka Iyotake's advice, and they did not hesitate to make their feelings known. They preferred action to words, and they said their chief was interfering and bossy. These young warriors had just questioned Tatanka Iyotake's position as a chief of the Lakota Nation and leader of the Strong Heart Society.

He dismounted his horse and took down his pipe bag and tobacco pouch. He proceeded to walk, with his noticeable limp, at a steady and deliberate pace toward the middle of the opposing force. When he had reached a point midway between the Lakota and the Long Knives, he sat down. He called back to the Lakota, inviting anyone who wished to smoke to join him and share his Cannupa. It was more of a challenge than an invitation.

None of the complainers stepped forward, including the warrior who claimed to be cloaked in invisibility and invulnerable to the Long Knives' guns. Only three men, two Cheyenne and Tatanka Iyotake's nephew White Bull, had the courage to join him. If there were any sharp-eyed observers, they would have noticed how shaky their legs were as they came and sat down.

When they sat down, Tatanka Iyotake proceeded to fill the pipe, and, with his flint and steel, he lit the pipe. He took some long leisurely puffs and passed it to his companions, who took smaller quick puffs. White Bull later said he hoped that if he took many quick puffs he could use up the tobacco faster. He was very aware of the clouds of dust kicked up by the bullets of the Long Knives' guns.

Once the pipe was finished, Tatanka Iyotake took out the tamping stick and cleaned the bowl. Neatly, he buried his ashes in the ground and put the pipe back in the pouch. Then he rose up slowly and started back at a measured pace toward his horse. He had not taken a few steps when the others rushed past him. One even left his weapons in his haste; he chose not to retrieve them.

When Tatanka Iyotake arrived back among the waiting Lakota warriors, he had humbled the warriors with his courage. Who had ever seen such an act of bravery? Words could not describe his fearlessness under such conditions. His action was incomparable. This time when he spoke and said the fighting is over, no one questioned his decision.

He further solidified his authority as a chief and leader with his action that day. Ultimately, the battle of Arrow Creek was indecisive and no one can claim victory; but the surveyors refused to venture back into that area again.

◈

BROKEN
PROMISES

Tatanka Iyotake's reputation grew among the Long Knives and the Wasicu. The Wasicu knew peace talks with him would be fruitless, just as Tatanka Iyotake knew the worthlessness of peace talks with the Wasicu. Then the Battle of the Yellowstone brought forth a Long Knife who would play a critical role in the future of the Lakota: Lieutenant Colonel George Armstrong Custer. A career military officer, Custer came west after the end of the American Civil War. His impact on the Lakota would be immense.

In the summer of 1874, Custer entered the Black Hills with 1,200 men, supposedly scouting locations for another fort to contain the Lakota. It has never been explained why that on a military surveying expedition, a number of nonmilitary personnel traveled with the soldiers. Among these were a geologist and two miners. They were seeking gold, and they found it.

The Black Hills are sacred lands for the Lakota. After what has been called Red Cloud's War in the late 1860s, the Treaty of 1868 had specifically set aside the Black Hills as Lakota territory forever. This was one of the strongest provisions in the treaty. The discovery of the Maza Zee (gold ore) made the Lakota claim to the Black Hills disappear, at least so far as white prospectors were concerned. Driven by gold fever, they swarmed into the area by the thousands.

Initially, the army made some desultory attempts to enforce the provisions of the treaty. They rounded up the trespassers and shipped them out of the Black Hills; but for each one taken away, another one or two slipped in. By January 1876, there were 15,000 miners in the Black Hills.

The army's enthusiasm for removing the miners was not high to begin with. General Sheridan ("Little Phil"), who was in charge of the army in the region, enforced the letter of the treaty, but made it known that if Congress decided to ignore the provisions of the treaty, he would be happier to protect the trespassers.

This is exactly what Congress decided to do. Having failed to uphold the treaty, the United States government decided on a forced purchase of the Black Hills from the Lakota. Red Cloud offered to agree to such a sale if the government would guarantee to support the Lakota for seven generations and pay $600,000,000. The government counter offered a $6,000,000 purchase price. When negotiations failed, Congress settled on a "fair offer" and presented it as an ultimatum. If the Lakota did not accept the government's terms, food supplies would be withheld until they were starved into submission.

In December 1875, during a bitterly cold winter, the agents and traders were ordered to stop selling ammunition to all Lakota. No one could hunt. The reservation agencies did not have sufficient food supplies. Hunger loomed ahead. The Lakota rebelled against the starvation of their children.

During that same winter, General "Three Stars" Crook was ranging the plains in pursuit of "hostile" Lakota—specifically Crazy Horse. When he finally located a winter village, he ordered an attack despite his scouts' report that it was not Crazy Horse's camp. As a result, Crook's forces destroyed the peaceful Cheyenne village of Chief Two Moons, killing men, women, and children. The survivors of this disaster found their way to Crazy Horse and then to Tatanka Iyotake's camp. The unprovoked attack on Two Moons' camp was a serious error by the Long Knives. It greatly angered the Cheyenne, who until this point had been uncommitted. Now they would stand with the Lakota against the American forces.

THE STAGE IS SET

When Tatanka Iyotake learned about the attack on Two Moons' camp, he was saddened; but he was not surprised. This act simply reconfirmed his belief that the Wasicu could not be trusted to keep their word and that war was inevitable. He sent messengers to every Lakota, Cheyenne, and Arapaho camp west of the Missouri River to come and join him in preparing to defend the homeland from the Long Knives. The call to join the leader of all the Lakota reached every camp, including the ones near the agencies. Jack Red Cloud, the son of Red Cloud, defied his father and joined Tatanka Iyotake. Warriors and their families started arriving at Tatanka Iyotake's camp at the Rosebud River in the spring of 1876.

Such a major undertaking required spiritual guidance. Tatanka Iyotake told the people he was going out alone to seek answers from Wakan Tanka. He crossed the Rosebud River and traveled a few miles to the northwest, where he located the right place to pray. He brought a buffalo skull, tobacco ties, and wakapa pi for offering.

Filling his Cannupa, he stood at the Hanblecheyapi altar and started singing prayer and Hanblecheyapi songs. He was seeking a location to hold the sacred Wiwang Wacipi. He prayed through the night and into the next day. Then, toward the evening of the second day, he saw two whirlwinds approaching. One was coming from the north, while the other was traveling from the south. The two whirlwinds merged in front of him. Looking into the whirlwinds, he saw a rock formation with a blue streak as if it had been struck by lightning.

When he finished his Hanblecheyapi, he returned to the camp. In just the short time he had been gone, the camp had grown considerably. More Lakota, Cheyenne, and Arapaho were arriving every day. They said they were guided by the four-legged and the winged to find the camp.

The camp started moving south along the Rosebud River. They had traveled and camped for two days when they came upon a cone butte, and the decision was made to camp beside it. They had an Inipi the first night, and some Cheyenne elders attended the Inipi. Tatanka Iyotake told of his vision. When he finished, the Cheyenne elders said they knew of this rock formation with the blue streak down the middle. It was a very sacred place to their people, and it was just a little farther down the Rosebud River. They called it the Deer Medicine Rocks.

The next morning Tatanka Iyotake climbed to the top of the cone butte. He filled his Cannupa and made a commitment to Wakan Tanka that he would perform the Wiwang Wacipi at this sacred place. He also prayed and said he would offer a whole buffalo and a red blanket.

The followers of Tatanka Iyotake traveled on and made camp

about five miles to the south of the Deer Medicine Rocks. Tatanka Iyotake invited his nephew White Bull to ride out with him on a hunt for buffalo. The pair soon killed three buffalo. Tatanka Iyotake selected the fattest of the three and asked White Bull to help him turn the cow on her stomach, with her chin on the ground. He then filled his Cannupa, offered the stem to the sky, and prayed. "Wakan Tanka, here is the whole buffalo I promised. In three days I will perform the Wiwang Wacipi and you will have the red blanket."

The preparations for the sacred ceremony began about one mile south of the Deer Medicine Rocks. The sixty-foot circular arena was ready, the cottonwood Wiwang Wacipi pole erected, and the sharp gravel spread throughout the arena. All was prepared. The people gathered around the perimeter of the circle and waited for Tatanka Iyotake to appear.

Three tipis had been set up: one for the singers, one for the council members, and finally one as a medicine lodge. Tatanka Iyotake was purifying himself in the Inipi ceremony. He had been fasting and preparing for his flesh offerings.

Finally, when he was ready, he entered the circle. His Hunka brother, the young Assiniboine now called Jumping Bull, walked at his side. Tatanka Iyotake wore his eagle bone whistle around his neck and an eagle feather in his unbraided hair. On his feet and hands he wore sage anklets and bracelets. His only clothing was a breechcloth made of buffalo hide, and for many of his supporters, this was the first time they had seen Tatanka Iyotake without a shirt. In silent awe, they observed a body covered with many scars from previous Wiwang Wacipi. He placed his filled Cannupa on the bleached buffalo skull, then went over and sat down with his back to the tree.

The singers began singing piercing songs as Tatanka Iyotake started praying by blowing his prayers through the eagle bone whistle. His Hunka brother, Jumping Bull, then began removing small pieces of flesh from Tatanka Iyotake's left shoulder. Jumping Bull continued until he had taken fifty pieces of flesh from each arm. After about thirty minutes, Tatanka Iyotake's offering of a "red blanket" was completed.

Bleeding profusely, Tatanka Iyotake rose and started to dance while gazing at the sun. The blood flowed freely down his arms. His feet, cut by the sharp gravel, left bloody marks on the ground.

The Wiwang Wacipi Wicasa continued his offering and his prayers. The sun sank below the horizon, but he danced on. The next morning he greeted the sun with the shrill of his eagle bone whistle. He continued to dance ceaselessly, staring at the sun, until noon, when his friend Black Moon ran to him and lowered his exhausted body to the ground.

Tatanka Iyotake spoke to Black Moon in muted tones. When the others came to tend to Tatanka Iyotake, Black Moon told the people his friend had had a vision. He said Wakan Tanka answered Tatanka Iyotake's prayers. Black Moon said his friend asked him to tell the people of his vision.

As Tatanka Iyotake danced, gazing at the sun, a voice spoke to him. The voice told him to look just below the sun. When he did, he saw many Long Knives falling into camp. They looked like grasshoppers with their feet above their heads and without ears. Below them were some natives also falling with their feet in the air and without ears. He heard the voice telling him, "I give you these Long Knives because they do not have ears. They will die, but do not take their belongings."

The Lakota interpreted Tatanka Iyotake's vision as a prediction of a great victory over the forces of the Wasicu who would not listen. Clearly, Wakan Tanka had spoken.

The camp had grown quite large by this time. Grass for the horses was getting scarce, and provisions for the people were running low. Scouts went in different directions to locate suitable pasturage for the horses and game to hunt.

The scouts who went west returned and reported an abundance of grass and an enormous herd of antelope around the valley of the greasy grass near the Little Big Horn River. The people broke camp and headed to the Little Big Horn River area, looking forward to feasting on antelope meat. They set up camp on the west side of the Little Big Horn River among the trees.

The hunts were successful, so the people feasted on antelope meat to celebrate a victory against the United States Army General they called "Three Stars" Crook. He was not a three-star general; but he did wear a star on each shoulder and one on his hat, so "Three Stars" he was. A few weeks earlier, Crazy Horse had led a contingent of Lakota and Cheyenne warriors against Crook's forces at the Rosebud River.

The warriors had shown their skills as the greatest equestrians of the Plains with their precision style of guerilla fighting on the back of a horse. They disrupted Crook's advance and forced him to retreat to Fort Fetterman. The army troops had expended 25,000 rounds of ammunition to kill a total of twenty Lakota and Cheyenne warriors. The soldiers, on the other hand, had ninety casualties, with nine soldiers and one Crow scout killed. The cavalry casualties would have been much higher if Crook had not ordered a retreat. Tatanka Iyotake told the people this was a great victory, but it was not the vision he had received at the Wiwang Wacipi.

Meanwhile, General Crook had reported his encounter with the Lakota and Cheyenne at the Rosebud River to his superior, General Alfred Terry. The style of fighting and level of confidence exhibited by the Lakota and Cheyenne had made Crook think there must be a great number of warriors. Any large gathering of warriors was alarming to the United States Army, so General Terry devised a plan of attack to counter this perceived threat.

The plan called for a three-pronged attack. Lieutenant Colonel Custer would proceed from Fort Abraham Lincoln in the east, moving westward to the Rosebud. General Gibbon would approach Tatanka Iyotake's camp from the west, and General Crook would come from the south. The plan was to surround the Lakota camp and destroy it by attacking simultaneously from all directions. The date for the attack was set for June 26, 1876.

Custer, however, believed the Lakota would be gone by June 26, so he devised a plan of his own. There has long been speculation that he felt a victory against the Lakota and Cheyenne would vault him into being the next president of the country. He knew his people elected heroes. A president is chosen based on his war victories and record, and his Seventh Cavalry could provide those victories for him.

Custer called in his Ree scouts (warriors from the Arikara tribe) and informed them of his decision to attack earlier than Terry had authorized. The scouts warned Custer that there were too many Lakota and Cheyenne in the valley of the Little Big Horn for his command of 750 men to defeat. Custer scoffed, "You boys always exaggerate the enemy's numbers!" He then proceeded to divide his 750 men into three battalions and set forth to meet his destiny.

Unaware of this, Tatanka Iyotake continued to ask the guidance of Wakan Tanka. He made some tobacco offerings. Then he crossed the Little Big Horn River and headed east to the top of the ridge now called Last Stand Hill. He selected a place to pray and put his offerings in a circle. He filled his Cannupa, sang a Thunder song, and prayed for the large gathering of Lakota, Cheyenne, and Arapaho camped just below. He prayed and asked that the people might live and that the spirits would protect and have pity on them. He finished his prayers, smoked his Cannupa, and then returned to camp. It was the evening of June 24, 1876.

◇

THE BATTLE OF THE GREASY GRASS

Custer assigned Captain Frederick Benteen 350 men and sent them to circle to the west of the Lakota camp. He assigned Major Marcus Reno 175 men and ordered them to approach from the south. Custer took the remaining 225 men to attack from the east.

Reno was the first to engage the Lakota when he charged the Hunkpapa camp. The first volley from his troops killed Chief Gall's two wives and his two daughters. The Hunkpapa warriors were quick to react, though, and repelled the attack. Reno ordered his troops to dismount at the edge of the tree line and form a skirmish line. Standing next to his Ree scout Bloody Knife, Reno prepared for the upcoming battle. Then a bullet from a Lakota rifle struck Bloody Knife in the head; blood and brains splattered all over Reno's head and clothes. Dazed and horrified, Reno called for an all-out retreat back across the river to the top of a hill. There he waited for Benteen to reinforce him.

Meanwhile, Custer led his 225 men under the cover of a deep ravine to the eastern edge of the Little Big Horn River. On the western side of the river, some young warriors were engaged in retrieving their horses. They spotted the column of soldiers on the east side of the river, getting ready to cross. The warriors were armed with rifles and started firing at this new troop of Long Knives. They picked off the first two riders in the file. The next two Long Knives reached down and picked up one of the fallen troopers, and the whole column turned and fled. The rout was on as they attempted to reach the top of the highest point to the northeast, a bluff now known as Last Stand Hill.

Tatanka Iyotake began preparing himself to join the battle. He was readying his favorite horse when his aged mother stopped him. She pointed out that he did not have to fight because he did not have anything more to prove to the people. She reminded him that he had two wives and small children to take care of. Since he was now a mature man of forty-five years, he could let the younger warriors prove their worth by protecting the camp and defending the people.

In the Lakota culture, the wisdom of women was much respected and admired. Tatanka Iyotake was a chief of the Lakota Nation and leader of the Midnight Strong Heart Society with many coups as a sash bearer, yet he had the ultimate respect for his mother's advice. He accepted her wisdom and bowed to her wishes by not participating in the battle. Instead, he guided the vulnerable noncombatants to a safe place.

The Long Knives were attempting to reach the highest point of the ridge. Gall was leading a group of warriors in pursuit when Crazy Horse and a band of Lakota came up over the top of the ridge and cut off the retreat. Two Moons and the Cheyenne warriors were coming in on the flanks. The shrill of the eagle bone whistles was just as loud as the constant sound of gunfire. The warriors were praying for help and guidance from the Spirits by blowing through their eagle bone whistles.

When the battle began, a young warrior was eager to join the fight and count coup. He had three good ponies, so he chose his favorite to ride into battle. He handed his weapons to a friend to hold while he caught the pony. Throwing a rope around its neck, he tried to mount; but the pony was excited, too. It shied and ran around in a circle at the end of the halter rope, with the young warrior chasing behind. By the time he had managed to catch the horse and mount, the battle was over. His brave plans to count coup on the enemy had disappeared while he tried to catch his horse. As one warrior said after the battle, "The fight with the Long Knives lasted as long as a hungry man eats his meal."

It was over that quickly.

The fact that Long Hair Custer was present was unknown to Tatanka Iyotake or to any of the Lakota, Cheyenne, and Arapaho warriors. Custer had cut his hair short and was dressed in the usual cavalry uniform rather than his flamboyant trademark buckskins. Unbeknownst to the Lakota warriors who had fired on the Long Knives at the river's edge, one of the two soldiers shot was Custer. He had been wounded and his men tried to protect and care for him. Custer was one of the first to fall at the Battle of the Greasy Grass.

When the fighting was over, Tatanka Iyotake rode through the battlefield and observed the aftermath. The fighting had ended at the very place where he had left his tobacco offerings the night before. He was proud to see his vision fulfilled, with the soldiers falling into camp upside down; but he was also very saddened because the people had not followed the vision. The voice in his vision had said for the people not to take the belongings of the Long Knives and not to scalp or mutilate the bodies. The people did not listen; and he knew the descendents of the Lakota, Cheyenne, and Arapaho Nations would suffer at the hands of the relatives of these Long Knives.

Tatanka Iyotake stood close to where he had prayed the night before and again filled his Cannupa. He began to pray for those who had fallen, including his own young son, the child of Red Woman, who had been kicked in the head and killed by a horse during the battle. He prayed for all the Lakota, Cheyenne, and Arapaho warriors who had died, but he also prayed for Custer and his men. He asked Wakan Tanka to receive the spirits of these warriors and Long Knives, for they had all fought bravely and honorably.

The victory celebrations were held in all areas of the large camp. There was much feasting and dancing, but it did not bring joy to Tatanka Iyotake. He was again in mourning for his son and saddened for the actions of the people. They had taken the spoils of battle, and in doing so, the people cursed their descendants. They would suffer under the Wasicu's laws, rules, and policies. The most devastating was when the Wasicu government created a law making it illegal for the Lakota people to live the ancient spiritual way of life. Everyone had freedom of religion in this country except the indigenous people.

In the Land of the Grandmother

The next few days after the battle were spent burying the dead, marking the areas where they had fallen, and preparing to scatter in different directions. Generals Gibbon and Crook were approaching.

Tatanka Iyotake told his friend Crazy Horse that he was going to take the Hunkpapa north to the land of the Grandmother, as the Lakota called Canada. He asked his friend to accompany him. Crazy Horse said he would decoy south and catch up to Tatanka Iyotake before he entered into Canada. The two friends never saw each other again in this life.

After parting from Crazy Horse, Tatanka Iyotake and his followers traveled north toward Canada. The people consisted of 135 lodges headed for the medicine line (the Canadian border). They altered their direction, and at times backtracked to confuse any pursuers, and they hoped for Crazy Horse to catch up to them.

Blackfoot Crowfoot (Glenbow Archives NA-1494-2)

Before they crossed the border, Tatanka Iyotake sent a courier carrying tobacco to the Blackfoot chief Crowfoot, asking Crowfoot to put aside their past differences and meet to forge an alliance against the Long Knives. Unfortunately, the Blackfoot occupied a hunting territory located mostly in Canada, and they had just completed a treaty with the Canadian government. Crowfoot refused Tatanka Iyotake's request. He even sent word to the Mounties about the presence of the Hunkpapa and offered his warriors to help fight them.

The Lakota, tired and hungry, crossed the medicine line and set up camp near a place called Pinto Horse Butte. It was May 1877. It was here that the Canadian Mounties found them and sent a small committee to have council. For this initial meeting, neither Tatanka Iyotake nor Major James Walsh, commanding officer of the Royal Canadian Mounted Police in this area, was present. Instead, Walsh's representatives met with Black Moon. The Canadians asked why the Hunkpapa had crossed the border and how long they intended to stay. Black Moon explained that they were asking refuge in the land of the Grandmother from Long Knives seeking vengeance after their defeat at the Battle of the Greasy Grass, this being the Lakota name for what the whites called Custer's Last Stand, or the Battle of the Little Big Horn in later years. Black Moon protested that the Lakota had not wanted to fight the Long Knives, but all efforts to make peace had resulted only in more broken promises, more violated treaties. The Lakota were requesting to be allowed to live here in peace.

This message was sent straightforward to Major Walsh. Finally, he agreed to meet with Tatanka Iyotake and the Hunkpapa. The first meeting, however, did not go well. Tatanka Iyotake, eager to find a new home for his people, pushed too hard for the cautious Canadian. The exchange became intense, and Walsh literally threw Tatanka Iyotake out of his office.

Later, when his temper cooled, Walsh reconsidered. He found that he could respect this strong, intelligent Hunkpapa leader, a man who so clearly cared deeply about the welfare of his people. Tatanka Iyotake, for his part, had found Walsh to be a man worthy of his respect. Based on their mutual regard, they established a long-term friendship. Walsh became a strong advocate for the refugee Lakota, but his relationship with Tatanka Iyotake was also a personal one. The two men found much to admire in each other. They shared knowledge with one another. Walsh taught Tatanka Iyotake to write his name in cursive script, using the English translation "Sitting Bull."

During this same time, Tatanka Iyotake also gained respect from the Blackfoot chief Crowfoot. Crowfoot accepted the presence of the Hunkpapa on the Blackfoot lands. His people shared their food and showed the Lakota where to hunt. In return, Tatanka Iyotake shared many gifts with Crowfoot. He taught the Blackfoot chief the sacred way of piercing in the Wiwang Wacipi and shared many other Lakota ceremonies with the Blackfoot tribe.

Crowfoot held the same position among the Blackfoot as Tatanka Iyotake held among the Lakota. Both were chiefs of their nations. As their mutual respect grew, Tatanka Iyotake felt moved to honor Crowfoot. To do this, he renamed his son after the Blackfoot Chief. This sign of respect from Tatanka Iyotake humbled Crowfoot.

General Nelson A. Miles, commander of the United States Army's forces in Missouri Territory, traveled to Canada to meet with Major Walsh. The purpose of his visit was to enlist Walsh's assistance in returning Tatanka Iyotake to the United States where they could take legal action against him for being the mastermind of Custer's defeat. Walsh refused. By this time, he had heard Tatanka Iyotake's side of the story and believed that the Lakota had been protecting their land and defending their spiritual way of life. Walsh did not want his friend "Bull" arrested based on what he considered a false accusation. This firm defense led the American newspapers to begin calling Walsh "Sitting Bull's Boss."

Major Walsh held to his decision to support Tatanka Iyotake and his people. His solution to the problem was to create a Canadian reserve (the equivalent of a tribal reservation in the United States) for the Lakota. The Canadian government, however, steadfastly refused.

The Lakota periodically slipped back across the United States border to hunt buffalo. One particular time the hunt was successful and about a hundred people, most of them women, were preparing the meat for transfer back to Canada. Tatanka Iyotake and his Hunka brother, Jumping Bull, were with the group.

Suddenly, one of the lookouts shouted that some strangers were approaching. These Natives had red flags attached to their rifles, so the Lakota thought they were asking to parley. What the Lakota did not know was that these riders were scouts for a column of Long Knives commanded by Lieutenant William Clarke. The red flags were to distinguish these Natives from any others for the benefit of the Long Knives; they were not a sign of wanting to parley.

The strangers came closer. Suddenly, without warning, they opened fire. Two Lakota warriors fell at once. The other Lakota shot back immediately, and as the exchange of bullets continued, the strangers were recognized as Crow, the longtime enemies of the Lakota. The rifle fire died down when a Crow warrior rode out between the opponents.

Major Walsh, Canadian Mounted Police (Library of Congress)

This warrior carried a white flag, and he did want to parley. A Lakota warrior rode out to speak to the Crow.

The Crow brave's message was a direct challenge to Tatanka Iyotake. There was a Crow warrior, he said, who wanted to meet Tatanka Iyotake in a personal fight. These two, as champions for their peoples, would decide who won and who lost this encounter.

Tatanka Iyotake had not had a fight in a while, so he was a little out of practice; but he had not lost any of his courage. Nor had he lost his knowledge of his responsibility as a leader of the Lakota. He knew that he had to meet and defeat this adversary to keep the people's confidence in his leadership. Tatanka Iyotake rode out to meet his opponent.

The Crow warrior had been eager for this opportunity to face Tatanka Iyotake. He had boasted that he could get rid of this troublesome Lakota for the Long Knives. As the two men rode toward each other, he raised his musket and shot. The musket misfired. The Crow was a large man, a fine target for Tatanka Iyotake's rifle. Tatanka Iyotake took aim and shot his challenger in the head. He rode over to the fallen body and took what scalp was left. Then he mounted the Crow's magnificent horse and rode back to the cheering Lakota warriors.

The Lakota had been in Canada for well over two years. Times were hard and people began to become discouraged. In the spring of 1879, some of the Hunkpapa started to slip away, reporting to various Indian agencies in the United States. The Canadian government felt as long as Walsh was near Tatanka Iyotake, he was not willing to return to the United States. They elected to transfer Walsh during the summer of 1879 to Fort Qu'Appelle in Saskatchewan. This caused great sadness for the two friends.

When Tatanka Iyotake learned that Walsh was leaving, he came to say goodbye to his friend. He entered Walsh's office wearing the magnificent headdress he was given when he was elected chief of the Lakota nation. Tatanka Iyotake spoke a formal farewell, reminding Walsh that the Lakota people were once strong and courageous with compassion for the land and all living things.

"Now, though," he said as he slipped off the headdress, "we are beggars and refugees from our homeland." "I want you to have this," he continued as he laid the headdress on the table. "Each eagle feather represents an act of bravery by the warrior who donated it." Then he left the room. Walsh was transferred shortly after that.

Even without the presence of Major Walsh, however, Tatanka Iyotake refused to return to the United States because Walsh had told him he was still trying to get him a reserve. Canadian officials persistently tried to persuade him to leave Canada. At the same time, they tried to persuade Walsh to ask his friend to go back. They were not willing to give the Lakota a reserve, so Walsh traveled to Washington, D.C., on behalf of Tatanka Iyotake. He was assured that Tatanka Iyotake would not be arrested or tried for Custer's defeat. Finally, in 1881, Walsh wrote a letter to his friend "Bull." He informed him to return to the United States without the fear of retaliation from the Long Knives.

Tatanka Iyotake, with 230 hungry Lakota, made the difficult journey toward Fort Buford, North Dakota. Arriving on July 20, 1881, they presented themselves to Major D. H. Brotherton. Tatanka Iyotake dismounted and handed his 1866 Winchester rifle to his son Crowfoot. The great Lakota chief spoke in sadness to the eight-year-old boy, "My son, if you live, you will not be a man, because you will not have a rifle

Ernie holding Sitting Bull's Winchester rifle (Family photograph)

or pony. Give my rifle to the Major and tell him I am the last Lakota to surrender."

Major Brotherton accepted the rifle and the surrender. Then he fed the hungry Lakota.

MILITARY CUSTODY

Brotherton immediately transferred the captured Lakota to the agency at Fort Yates, North Dakota. However, they were confined to protected custody at Fort Randall, South Dakota, in September 1881. The United States government said the reason for this was that Tatanka Iyotake's life might be in danger from his own people. The government was actually more inclined to believe Tatanka Iyotake still posed a threat to them, and that was the real reason for his confinement. The 25th Infantry, a regiment consisting of black enlisted men (buffalo soldiers) and white officers, put the Lakota under guard.

Among the prisoners was a group of warriors from the Midnight Strong Heart Society who were especially close to Tatanka Iyotake. They had formed an alliance, calling themselves the Silent Eaters. The Silent Eaters had vowed to protect Tatanka Iyotake at all costs. They swore to step in front of a bullet or arrow to protect him and to fight to the death for him. In just a few years, some of these men would die upholding their oath.

While incarcerated at Fort Randall, Tatanka Iyotake became

Sitting Bull at Fort Randall, 1882 (Family photograph)

acquainted with the wife of the post quartermaster, Captain Horace Quimby, who was from New Hampshire. When transferred to South Dakota, he had brought with him his wife, Martha, and their two daughters, eighteen-month-old Belle and five-year-old Alice. His wife's sister, Margaret Smith, also relocated to South Dakota with the Quimby family. Martha Quimby, her sister Margaret, and her daughter Alice visited the Hunkpapa camp. They soon became friends with Tatanka Iyotake's family, usually bringing gifts and food. Martha Quimby later claimed to have taught Tatanka Iyotake to write his name as "Sitting Bull"; but, of course, James Walsh had already taught him when he was in Canada. However, he may have chosen to pretend not to know how to write his name in cursive. Such a small act of kindness would have been completely in character.

On one visit, Martha noticed Tatanka Iyotake had made a sketch from his winter count ledger, drawn on buffalo hide for the Indian

z

s

From left to right: twin boy, Alice Quimby, twin boy, Four Robes with baby girl, Sitting Bull, Margaret Smith, Captain Quimby on horse at Fort Randall, 1882 (Family photograph)

MILITARY CUSTODY

agent. The accounts were in chronological order and showed special events and accomplishments in his life. She asked him if he would draw some for her, and he readily agreed. He was particularly fond of her daughter Alice, and this was possibly the reason why he agreed to Martha's request. Tatanka Iyotake was very fond of children. Martha brought a ledger book she had gotten from the Indian agent, and with some colored pencils, Tatanka Iyotake started drawing and coloring some of his accounts. He picked random events for the drawings he did for her.

Tatanka Iyotake had completed twelve drawings for Martha before the Quimbys were transferred to another post in 1882. The day the Quimbys were boarding a steamboat, Tatanka Iyotake presented the thirteenth drawing to Martha. It was an unfinished picture of a horse without a rider.

When Captain Quimby died in 1883, his wife, Martha, and children then moved to Niles, Michigan. Martha passed away thirteen years later after slipping on an icy sidewalk and fracturing her skull. Alice Quimby inherited the drawings, and when she passed away in 1947, they were given to the Fort St. Joseph Museum in Niles, Michigan. The collection of original pictographs is on display at the museum today.

A LIMITED CAPTIVITY

Tatanka Iyotake and the Hunkpapa Lakota left Fort Randall in April 1883 and were transferred to the Standing Rock Indian Reservation. When they arrived, the division within the Hunkpapa Nation was already evident. Many of the staunchest supporters of Tatanka Iyotake during the 1870s had accepted the ways of the Wasicu and their Christian religion. The Indian agent James McLaughlin declared Tatanka Iyotake a hostile obstructionist because of his stance and his belief in the traditional Lakota way of life. McLaughlin said Tatanka Iyotake was a bad influence because he opposed sending his children to the agency school. He blamed him for the poor attendance at the school. This was just one item in a long list of complaints McLaughlin had about Tatanka Iyotake.

Called "White Hair" by the Lakota, McLaughlin administered Standing Rock with a jealous eye on anyone who threatened his authority. All too frequently, the challenges came from Tatanka Iyotake, who refused to bow to McLaughlin. "White Hair" came to dislike the strong influence the chief of the Lakota Nation had over the

Hunkpapa, because many times during meetings, if Tatanka Iyotake did not like the topic, he simply stood up and walked out, and almost all the tribal council members followed him out the door. Tatanka Iyotake did not understand why this Wasicu wanted power and control over the people.

By this time, Tatanka Iyotake was truly famous. People all over the world knew his name and invited him to public events. McLaughlin could not keep his high-profile prisoner out of the public eye. He may also have been shrewd enough to realize that the more often Tatanka Iyotake was absent from the reservation, the easier it was for him to control the rest of the Hunkpapa.

Tatanka Iyotake was invited to the Dakota Territory celebration declaring Bismarck the capital of North Dakota. This event included the president of the United States, Chester Arthur, and Tatanka Iyotake was informed he could have council with him. He did not have a meeting with the president as promised, but instead he was asked to give a speech to the citizens of Bismarck. He did not speak Wasicu, so he spoke in Lakota, and the officials of the event provided a translator to translate his speech into Wasicu. When Tatanka Iyotake stood up and addressed the crowd, the translator was shocked about what he said. He did not say any nice things; instead, he told the people of Bismarck what a disgrace they were to his people and the coveting and destroying of the land. When he finished his speech, the translator stood up and delivered a pre-written speech. When he finished, the people gave Tatanka Iyotake a standing ovation. While there, the chief of staff for Chester Arthur presented a J. G. Volz & Co. beaver felt top hat in exchange for his autograph. It was customary for the government to give these beaver felt top hats to noted chiefs and political leaders of certain Native tribes.

It so happened that there was a showman in the audience that day, and he noted the ovation given to Tatanka Iyotake. This man's name was Alvaren Allen, and he saw what he thought was a moneymaking performance. Allen asked Indian agent McLaughlin for permission for Tatanka Iyotake to be part of his show. He was allowed to include Tatanka Iyotake in his show under the heading of "Sitting Bull Connection." The show toured mostly in southern Canada and parts of the northern United States. The show was touring in St. Paul, Minnesota, when a petite dark-haired girl was also there performing a shooting exhibition. She was with a variety show that included many different kinds of performers. Tatanka Iyotake was in the audience and was impressed with her shooting skills. The young woman was Phoebe Ann Mosey, better known as Annie Oakley. She reminded Tatanka Iyotake of his daughter, Walks Looking, who was not with him on the tour. He requested to meet with her, and after the meeting, he verbally "adopted" her. He gave her a Lakota name, Watanya Cikala, which means Little Sure Shot. He also gave her a pair of beaded moccasins as a gift for her as his newly "adopted" daughter.

Agent McLaughlin only allowed Alvaren Allen one tour with Tatanka Iyotake, but during that tour, William F. Cody heard of the successful venture. He also requested Tatanka Iyotake, and had him join his Wild West show. Tatanka Iyotake took the beaver felt top hat with him when William F. Cody took him on his Buffalo Bill Cody's Wild West Show from June 1885 to October 1885. The Wild West Show toured throughout the United States. Tatanka Iyotake rode in

Showmen in Buffalo Bill's Wild West Show, 1885 (Family photograph)

parades and greeted visitors in his tipi. They introduced him during the show as "the killer of Custer," and he was greeted with disrespect at every stop. Yet, at every location, people lined up to meet him and paid to get autographs. He was a very popular attraction.

When the show ended on October 3, Cody gave him a white hat with a monarch butterfly on the front of the hatband. True to his humility and generous way, Tatanka Iyotake gave his J. G. Volz & Co. beaver felt top hat to an employee at a hotel in St. Louis. Serle Chapman purchased the hat at an auction in 2005 and returned it to the great-grandson of Tatanka Iyotake in June 2006.

Modern historians and scholars tried to contradict Tatanka Iyotake's belief by saying that he opposed the Wasicu way of life, yet he

Sitting Bull's beaver felt top hat (Family photograph)

lived in a log cabin and sold his autograph for two dollars. But the log cabin belonged to his brother-in-law Grey Eagle, who had accepted the Wasicu way of life, and during the time he spent with Cody, Tatanka Iyotake gave away all the money he made for his autographs to the ragged little white children begging on the streets. This is one thing he never understood, how the white people could neglect their children. In the Lakota language, children are called *Wakayaja* or *Wakan Icaga* (something sacred is growing). The Lakota nurtured and took special care of the children. The people always cared for them. They were educated in the sacred ways of the Lakota and taught not to be beggars but to be providers and take care of each other. Tatanka Iyotake knew the future of the Lakota children had a bleak outlook if the people followed the Wasicu example in neglecting their children.

In October of 1888, McLaughlin allowed Tatanka Iyotake to

travel with a delegation of Lakota chiefs to Washington, D.C. During his visit, Tatanka Iyotake gave an interview about his vision of the Battle of the Little Big Horn and the structure of the Midnight Strong Heart Society. He told the reporters about the role of the Midnight Strong Heart Society. The society elected members because of their high regard for being compassionate and courageous with high integrity yet humble. They were the protectors and the providers for the tribe, and they taught by example. He spoke about an alliance created within the society, the fellowship of individuals that called their group the Silent Eaters. They vowed to protect and/or die fighting for their chief against all aggressors.

Delegation at Washington, D.C., 1888. Sitting Bull, standing slightly apart, is the first person on the left of the third row from the bottom (Library of Congress)

THE GHOST DANCE

B y the end of the 1880s, the Lakota were a broken people without any hope for the future. It was at this time that a Northern Paiute holy man named Wovoka (aka Jack Wilson) brought hope to the natives across the land. His father was a well-known holy man with a title as a "Weather Doctor." He had sent his son Jack to follow his example and to also learn to be a "Weather Doctor." It was during this training period that Jack experienced a vision. On January 1, 1889, there was a solar eclipse, and during this eclipse, he fell into a trance. Jack said he stood before God and saw most of his friends and ancestors engaging in their favorite pastimes. He said God instructed him to tell his people to love one another and to live in peace with the white people. God also told him to advise the people they must work, not fight, steal, or lie. God said if the people abided by these rules, they would unite with friends and family members in the other world. Jack proclaimed there would not be any sickness, disease, or old age. He received the "Ghost Dance" to take back to the people.

The new religion was termed "Dance in a Circle." The first contact white people had with the Ghost Dance came by the way of the Lakota; their reference was the "Spirit Dance," and it subsequently was translated as the Ghost Dance. Most Natives of the western portion of the United States sent delegates to investigate the self-proclaimed prophet and his religion; even the Mormons from Utah sent investigators. Some followers also believed in a Ghost Shirt. These shirts were rumored to repel bullets through spiritual power. It is uncertain where the concept of the Ghost Shirt originated, but it is thought that there is a possible connection to the Mormon endowment "garment," which the Mormons believe would protect the wearer from danger. Kicking Bear and Short Bull brought the concept to the Lakota with their interpretation of Jack's religion. They told the Lakota that if they practiced the Ghost Dance diligently, there would be a renewed Earth in which all evil was washed away and all the white people would be removed. They also told the people all their friends and relatives who were killed by the white people would return to life and all the buffalo would return in abundance. This was not Jack's version of his vision, which stated a harmonious coexistence with the white people.

Kicking Bear was a Minneconjou Lakota who believed in the Ghost Dance. He arrived at Standing Rock Indian Reservation in early 1890. Tatanka Iyotake still followed the traditional Lakota spiritual ways. He did not believe in the religion, but he allowed Kicking Bear to teach the people around him. He did not object or interfere when they accepted the beliefs and began to practice this dance. He knew the people needed something to help them survive and gain hope for the future.

McLaughlin, however, started to worry about the influence this was having on the Lakota camp on the Grand River. He thought the Ghost

Dance religion was starting to help Tatanka Iyotake regain his standing among the Hunkpapa. McLaughlin had repeatedly told Tatanka Iyotake that he could not do anything without permission from him. Once again, Tatanka Iyotake was flouting McLaughlin's authority.

Meanwhile, Tatanka Iyotake had also realized the Ghost Dance was overpowering the people. Instead of giving them hope for the future and strength to endure the present, it was taking over their lives. He wondered how the other leaders were dealing with it. He went out on the prairie to pray and to receive inspiration from Wakan Tanka. As he was returning to his cabin, he encountered a Tasiyagnupa (meadowlark), one of his special winged messengers. The meadowlark spoke a warning to him, saying, "The Lakota will kill you."

This was in August of 1890. Despite the meadowlark's warning, Tatanka Iyotake felt he could not abandon his people. He had to try to get them to realize that the dance could not provide what it promised; he had to try without throwing them back into despair and hopelessness.

BETRAYAL

The white man's tactic of divide and conquer was working well among the Hunkpapa. Many of Tatanka Iyotake's faithful followers and supporters in his fight for the Lakota way of life had turned to the Wasicu way. They had also accepted the Wasicu religion and abandoned the sacred pipe and the ceremonies. These actions saddened Tatanka Iyotake because members of his own extended family had turned away from the ancient ways and teachings of the Hunkpapa Lakota.

McLaughlin had been successful in convincing many of those under his supervision at Standing Rock that they should settle down and give up the nomadic lifestyle of the Lakota. However, he had little faith in his ability to convince Tatanka Iyotake to become a farmer. The old Lakota leader's determination to continue the old ways worried and frustrated McLaughlin. To keep Tatanka Iyotake and his family under control, McLaughlin recruited an informer to observe every decision they made. This included infiltrating even the closest circles around Tatanka Iyotake.

The Silent Eaters within the Midnight Strong Heart Society were staunch in their support. Tatanka Iyotake was intrigued, though, by the way McLaughlin seemed always to know what was spoken in his council meetings. Obviously, at least one council member was not what he pretended to be, a friend or relative of Tatanka Iyotake. The meetings' main topic was usually the Ghost Dance religion, and McLaughlin always knew what was discussed and decided.

On December 14, 1890, Tatanka Iyotake had council with the Silent Eaters and the elders, and announced he was going to travel to the Pine Ridge Indian Reservation to confer with Red Cloud. He felt it was time to address the issues arising from the Ghost Dance. Although McLaughlin had told Tatanka Iyotake that he could not travel anywhere without permission, Tatanka Iyotake told the council members that he was a Lakota, free to travel on the land without permission from anyone.

How did McLaughlin learn of this plan? That question has been asked many times over the decades. This is the answer.

Present at the council, as always, was One Bull. He was the son of Tatanka Iyotake's older sister, Good Feather Woman. He always attended the meetings, since Tatanka Iyotake had accepted the responsibility for his nephew's education, just as Four Horns had done with him. He tried to share with One Bull similar things to what he learned from Four Horns. One Bull, though, had chosen a different path. He had chosen to be the informer for agent McLaughlin. He attended all the council meetings and listened carefully about the decisions and plans they agreed on. He then slipped away to the present-day community of Little Eagle to the Wasicu schoolteacher, who had access to a telegraph. He told him all the details of the

Sitting Bull and One Bull, 1885—note how Sitting Bull is dressed in the
traditional way and One Bull is dressed as a white man (Serle Chapman)

meeting, and the teacher would send the message to McLaughlin by telegraph. After the meeting on the evening of December 14, 1890, One Bull learned the telegraph office was closed on Sunday, but he had to get the results of the meeting to Fort Yates, North Dakota. He slipped away from his uncle's council and quickly rode his horse to McLaughlin's office in Fort Yates. He told McLaughlin that Tatanka Iyotake was preparing his horse for fast travel to Pine Ridge, disobeying McLaughlin's order. One Bull then rode his exhausted horse to death, racing back toward Tatanka Iyotake's camp. He ran the rest of the way, trying to get back to his tipi before the Indian police arrived so as not to be discovered as the informer. He was a policeman under the command of McLaughlin and was the informer in Tatanka Iyotake's council meetings. The murder of Tatanka Iyotake and his son along with his close associates, the Silent Eaters, was a tragedy caused by the betrayal of his nephew, One Bull.

Two very important pieces of written evidence support what the descendents of Tatanka Iyotake have always known about the role of One Bull. The first of these is a letter from E. D. Mossman, superintendent of the Standing Rock Indian School, to the Commissioner of Indian Affairs in Washington, D.C., dated August 25, 1922. [To view complete letter, see Appendix 1]. It states:

> For your information, I will say that Sitting Bull has practically no relatives on this reservation. His nearest of kin now living here are One Bull, a nephew, and the wife of Grey Eagle. One Bull, while his nephew, was one of the men who went as police to arrest Sitting Bull at the time of his death.

The second piece of evidence comes from the mouth of One Bull himself. When he was interviewed after the murder, One Bull first claimed that he was "away from home" when his uncle was killed. As reported in *The Arrest and Killing Of Sitting Bull*, edited by John Carroll, a second version of his testimony states:

> Late in the night McLaughlin and Louis Primeau came to me and said: "No matter where the ghost dancers go, you and your uncle had better remain where you are. The soldiers from the Heart River, Slim Buttes, and Fort Sully are coming."
>
> I left the Agency very early in the morning and as one of my horses was played out, I was delayed on the way and did not reach my home until about daybreak the next morning. (p. 96)

To the end of her days, Tatanka Iyotake's daughter, Standing Holy (Mary Sitting Bull-Spotted Horse), held One Bull directly responsible for her father's death. In the year 1917, Standing Holy and three of her children were traveling to Standing Rock to visit some relatives. One of her children was fourteen-year-old Angelique, who later became the mother of Ernie LaPointe. The family was traveling by wagon, and the journey was long and tiring.

When they were well inside the Standing Rock Reservation, a man on horseback approached from the opposite direction. As he neared the wagon, Standing Holy took her shawl and covered her head. The man rode up to the wagon and greeted the family cheerfully. He asked about Standing Holy's family, their health and well-being. Standing Holy replied from under her shawl. She told the man to move on, that

Standing Holy, 7 years old, 1883 (Family photograph)

Standing Holy, 1883 (Family photograph)

she did not want to look at his face ever again. She said that it was because of his secret actions, spying, and informing for the Indian police and Agent McLaughlin that they came and killed her father. She told him her family knew he had ridden to Fort Yates the day before Tatanka Iyotake was murdered to tell agent McLaughlin of Tatanka Iyotake's plan to travel to Pine Ridge to have council with Red Cloud. Then he had ridden his horse to death returning to camp before the Indian police arrived, because he did not want to be discovered as the camp informant. When Standing Holy finished, the man replied by telling her she should not be saying that, but Standing Holy refused to change her words. He eventually rode on.

Angelique asked her mother who the man was. Standing Holy told her his name was Henry Oscar One Bull. She told her daughter always to beware of him and his family, because the reward for his betrayal of her father was recognition by McLaughlin as a true, faithful, obedient servant to the Wasicu government. The actions of One Bull, the Indian police, and all their supporters had put a curse on their own descendants because they killed the true chief of the Tiatunwa Lakota, and more importantly, they had killed a Sun Dancer.

In the Lakota way, this tragic event must be made right within four generations, and if it isn't, it will never be. Ernie LaPointe and his three sisters are the third generation.

The Murder

The historical accounts of the death of Tatanka Iyotake present us with a narrative that flows smoothly from point to point, often glossing over some glaring discrepancies. These accounts are from a single source: Stanley Vestal (Walter Campbell), who, in 1930, came to the Standing Rock Sioux Reservation to look for descendents of Tatanka Iyotake. Wanting to write a biography of Tatanka Iyotake, he interviewed One Bull. The accounts provided by One Bull are not accurate. One Bull adopted Walter Campbell as his son so Campbell would not doubt his story.

To make their father more credible, One Bull's daughters fabricated the story that he was adopted as a son by Tatanka Iyotake through the Hunkayapi Ceremony. No Lakota person would go through the Hunkayapi Ceremony with a person who is already a blood relative. Tatanka Iyotake had acted as a mentor to his sister's son in the same way that his father's brother Four Horns had taught him.

Stanley Vestal never spoke to any of the direct descendents of Tatanka Iyotake. Vestal believed the words of One Bull and penned the book *Sitting Bull, Champion of the Sioux* from One Bull's accounts. Every book author and historian since that time has treated this novel as an historical document, but in reality, it is a work of fiction.

The story of the death of Tatanka Iyotake, written by and from the point of view of a non-Lakota, does not correspond to the reports of three eyewitnesses to the event. These witnesses were the children of Tatanka Iyotake, who were present when their father was murdered.

Ernie LaPointe's mother learned these stories from her mother, Standing Holy, and from her uncles, John Sitting Bull and Henry Little Soldier. Standing Holy was the youngest daughter of Tatanka Iyotake and Seen by Her Nation. John Sitting Bull, whose Lakota name was Refuses Them, was a deaf-mute and was the son of Seen by Her Nation. Henry Little Soldier was the son of Four Robes. Seen by Her Nation and Four Robes had both been married to Bear Louse before they married Tatanka Iyotake, and each had a son from their first marriage. Tatanka Iyotake treated the boys as his own. They were present when Tatanka Iyotake was murdered on the morning of December 15, 1890. Their story is quite different from the One Bull version.

All accounts agree that forty-three Metal Breasts (Indian police) came to the sleeping camp of Tatanka Iyotake in the early morning hours of December 15. From that point on, however, the accounts diverge. Some of the more dramatic reports say that the police burst into the cabin and forced Tatanka Iyotake from his bed, then dragged the naked elder out into the yard. Since it was a December winter morning, this seems highly unlikely.

Instead, according to his stepsons, the police knocked on the door and asked him to come outdoors. They waited for him while he got dressed, putting on his shirt and leggings. In support of this, the

Smithsonian Institution has returned to Ernie LaPointe (in December 2007) the leggings taken off the corpse of Tatanka Iyotake.

Inside the cabin were Tatanka Iyotake's wives and children, including his two stepsons and his son Crowfoot. Crowfoot was a young man of seventeen at that time, not a fourteen-year-old boy, as is often reported. When Tatanka Iyotake walked toward the door of the cabin, Crowfoot also jumped up and picked up his weapon. He told his father he would protect him. "I will stand with you."

At the door, Tatanka Iyotake paused, then turned around and sang a farewell song to his family. He sang, "I am a man and wherever I lie is my own." As he turned and stepped out the door, Crowfoot walked behind him carrying his weapon. Those inside the cabin said it seemed like forever when gunfire erupted. Tatanka Iyotake fell in front of the door, and a few seconds later Crowfoot fell next to his father. Six Silent Eaters of the Midnight Strong Heart Society died along with their friend, chief, and Sun Dancer that cold December morning.

Here is a final discrepancy in the story. Many reports, especially those of the surviving Indian police, said that Crowfoot was hiding under a bed in the cabin. The police hauled him out, crying and pleading for his life. Bull Head, the leader of the Indian police, ordered Crowfoot's death, and his police officers killed the boy. This is similar to the fabricated story of Tatanka Iyotake being dragged naked into his yard; it seeks to humiliate the memory of his son.

Crowfoot died outside the cabin. There was a crying child present, but it was twelve-year-old William. His older half-brother, Crowfoot, had already died with his father. It is not too hard to understand why the boy was afraid for his life. The other story is a complete fabrication.

Crowfoot, 10 years old, 1883 (Family photograph)

The immediate family members were all horrified witnesses to the death of Tatanka Iyotake. As the United States Army unit assigned to back up the Indian police moved into the camp, the family and other residents fled for their lives. Now there were not only the Metal Breasts to fear, but also the soldiers. Tatanka Iyotake's two wives, Seen by Her Nation and Four Robes, took their five children and Tatanka Iyotake's oldest daughter, Many Horses, and headed south. The children included Tatanka Iyotake's stepsons, John Sitting Bull (Refuses Them) and Henry Little Soldier. Tatanka Iyotake's biological children were Standing Holy (Mary Sitting Bull), daughter of Seen by Her Nation, as well as Lodge in Sight (Lizzie Sitting Bull) and Runs Away From (William Sitting Bull), children of Four Robes.

As they fled across the Grand River, the family and about 200 other members of the camp were intercepted by Army forces, which were sent in pursuit. They were put under protective custody at Fort Yates. The males ranging from sixteen to fifty years of age were incarcerated at Fort Sully until the spring of 1891. McLaughlin feared the Strong Heart Society, and he assumed these males were part of the society and would retaliate for the death of Tatanka Iyotake.

Even the army had been a bit surprised at the intensity of the reaction by the other Hunkpapa against Tatanka Iyotake's family. Many of the people were angry because their loved ones had died in the process of arresting Tatanka Iyotake. In one case, a father and son fought against each other—the son on the side of the police and the father with his old friend, the chief. By this time, many of the Hunkpapa had relented to the demands of McLaughlin and wanted to be "good Indians." They had adopted Christianity and they followed the white man's way. Tatanka Iyotake opposed the white man's way of life. He and his followers wanted to be left alone to the live the old way. This rift within the Hunkpapa was devastating. It is more than a little ironic that the United States Army became the guardians of the family of one of their most steadfast opponents, protecting them from their own people.

107
◈

Burying
the Dead

Freighter James Hanson delivering goods to Fort Yates, North Dakota, had his wagon commandeered by Colonel Fechet and was ordered to accompany his troops to the Grand River area of South Dakota. They were to retrieve the bodies of the "Sioux" Indian policemen and the body of Tatanka Iyotake. When the party arrived at the cabin of Tatanka Iyotake, they were horrified at the condition of the Wiwang Wacipi Wicasa and chief of the Lakota Nation. The relatives of the policemen killed during the failed arrest attempt had beaten him virtually unrecognizable. Hanson drove the bodies of Tatanka Iyotake and the policemen to Fort Yates, North Dakota.

The post surgeon, Dr. Horace M. Deeble, received the battered body of Tatanka Iyotake at 4:30 p.m. on December 16, 1890. Dr. Deeble was the acting post coroner/mortician. He performed a postmortem examination on the body of Tatanka Iyotake. He reported to Agent McLaughlin that Tatanka Iyotake had a gunshot wound in the left side between the tenth and eleventh ribs and that the bullet traveled down

The Grand River, just a few feet from Sitting Bull's cabin (Serle Chapman)

toward the pelvis without an exit. He also reported a gunshot wound in the right cheek just below the right eye. McLaughlin possibly gave a verbal order not to perform an autopsy on the body, so the bullets are buried with Tatanka Iyotake. The order did not apply to the other items belonging to Tatanka Iyotake, and Dr. Deeble took possession of the blood-saturated leggings and cut off the small braid from the scalp lock. The small braid held the Hunkpapa Lakota chief's eagle feathers. Dr. Deeble wrapped the naked body of Tatanka Iyotake in a canvas bag, put it in a pine box, and buried him unceremoniously in the post cemetery. He posted sentries around the grave to prevent the relatives of the Indian policemen and the agency "Indians" from desecrating the remains of Tatanka Iyotake.

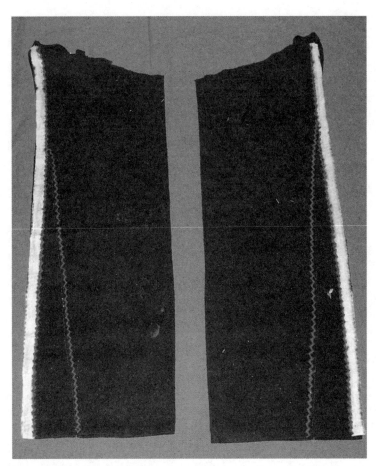

Sitting Bull's leggings (Family photograph)

The surviving people who had fled after the murders did not return to the camp to bury the six Silent Eaters and Seen by Her Nation's son Crowfoot for fear of retaliation from the agency "Indians" and agent McLaughlin. Instead, the families and friends of these seven men came quietly, under cover of night, and changed their clothing to make them presentable for their journey to the Spirit World. It was difficult knowing their loved ones were not going to have a sacred ceremony and burial, but the hostility against them was so great that any effort to bury them with honor was dangerous.

The bodies remained where they fell. It was approximately a week later that Reverend Riggs, a teacher at the Peoria Flats divinity school next to Fort Sully, learned these men did not receive a proper burial. He immediately set out to correct the situation. He asked one of his students to travel with him to the scene of the neglected bodies and prepare them for burial.

When they arrived at the scene, they found there was both good news and bad news. The bodies were properly dressed, and because of the cold December temperatures, were still preserved. However, the ground was frozen and digging even one grave would require more men. The pair traveled to Fort Yates to try to recruit help from some of the agency "Indians." Naturally, they tried to enlist the help of the relatives and friends of the deceased men. They learned the relatives and friends feared for their lives if they tried to give any proper ceremony for their loved ones. The reverend could not convince any of the relatives and friends to help.

Finally, Reverend Riggs had to resort to bribery. He promised the agency "Indians" they could have Tatanka Iyotake's chickens, pigs, and a cow as payment for digging the graves. There were twelve agency "Indians," certainly not acting with the respect for the dead that a true Lakota would show, who were willing to travel to the site and help with the digging and burying for pay. It was a two-to-three day ordeal, but they dug a mass grave. Crowfoot was the first one in the grave.

When the burial was complete, the reverend lived up to his promise. He allowed the agency "Indians" to take the chickens and other animals belonging to Tatanka Iyotake. Then the group returned to Fort Yates with news of the burial of the traditional Hunkpapa Lakota. The response to this was truly shocking. The whole tribe prepared a powwow to celebrate the event! They feasted and danced, shouting, "Now all the evildoers are dead and buried."

Now they could become Wasicu and accept his Christian religion and ways without any further interruptions from individuals living the Lakota spiritual way of life. James McLaughlin taught the Standing Rock Indians to be faithful obedient servants to the Great White Father in Washington, D.C. They still despise the memory of Tatanka Iyotake and his living lineal descendents.

LEAVING
STANDING
ROCK

In June of 1891, a Spirit came to Seen by Her Nation and told her to prepare her family for fast travel. The Spirit told her they would be guided away from Standing Rock Indian Reservation and the Indian agent James McLaughlin. The reason for the move away from Standing Rock was to preserve the heritage and bloodline of Tatanka Iyotake.

At dawn of the next morning, the family along with about 200 Hunkpapa, slipped away. A Tasiyagnupa guided them to the Cheyenne River. They came to the Badlands of South Dakota through present-day Red Shirt Table. They stayed close to the western edge of the Badlands. There were lookouts posted at various locations to warn about the approach of strangers. When a stranger approached, the people slipped into the Badlands. For nearly a year, their presence went undetected.

It was in the spring of 1892 when the Indian agent at the Pine

Taken not long after Sitting Bull's death—Lodge in Sight, Four Robes, Seen By Her Nation, and Standing Holy, 1890 (Family photograph)

Ridge Agency discovered this large group of Hunkpapa living within the boundaries of the reservation. He brought them to the agency and had them enrolled into the Pine Ridge Indian Reservation. They were granted land allotments around the area where they had been camped.

The people of Standing Rock Indian Reservation were happy the descendents of Tatanka Iyotake left and became enrolled at the Pine Ridge Indian Reservation. Tatanka Iyotake's first wife, Seen by Her Nation, passed away in 1897 without ever going back to Standing Rock Indian Reservation. Her own brother, Gray Eagle, and her nephew, One Bull, had betrayed her. For her, this was unforgivable.

Four Robes, Tatanka Iyotake's second wife, however, wanted to return to Standing Rock Indian Reservation. She missed her brother, Gray Eagle, and his family. In 1900, she sent her son Runs Away From (William Sitting Bull) to Standing Rock Reservation to seek

Gray Eagle, his wife, baby Moses, and son Clarence, 1903 (Family photograph)

enrollment. Runs Away From's request was denied in 1908 by the Tribal Government of Standing Rock. Their reason was they did not want the son of a troublemaker enrolled in the tribe. He returned to Pine Ridge and passed away in 1909 at the age of thirty-one.

This is proof there are not any direct lineal descendents of Tatanka Iyotake living or enrolled at Standing Rock, despite claims made by the One Bull family. They claimed to be lineal descendents of Tatanka Iyotake. In reality, they are collateral relatives, not descendents at all. Since the Lakota people counted family bilineally, meaning that both the father's and the mother's family were ancestors of a person, only those who are the children of Tatanka Iyotake and his wives are descendents. One Bull, the son of Tatanka Iyotake's older sister, could claim to be a descendent of Tatanka Iyotake's parents; but that is the extent of the relationship.

Standing Holy, Seen By Her Nation, Runs Away From, Lodge In Sight, Four Robes, 1891 (Family photograph)

The descendents of One Bull still do not want to accept the lineal descendents of Tatanka Iyotake. Their argument states that when the family of Tatanka Iyotake left the Standing Rock Indian Reservation, they left their bloodline and relationship to Tatanka Iyotake there. This is a strange argument. They seem to assume that descent is based on location rather than blood.

THE BURIAL SITE OF TATANKA IYOTAKE

Tatanka Iyotake was the only person still buried in the old military cemetery at Fort Yates, North Dakota, for years after his death. The people of Standing Rock Indian Reservation ignored the grave for sixty-three years. The state of North Dakota and the federal government also neglected the burial site of a Wiwang Wacipi Wichasha and the true chief of the Lakota Nation.

In 1953, Tatanka Iyotake's three granddaughters decided to move their grandfather's remains away from Fort Yates. They were hoping to achieve success in getting their grandfather a respectful resting place. The granddaughters were Angelique Spotted Horse-LaPointe, Sarah Spotted Horse-Little Spotted Horse, and Nancy Sitting Bull-Kicking Bear. Angelique and Sarah were daughters of Standing Holy (Mary Sitting Bull) and Nancy was the daughter of Runs Away From (William Sitting Bull). Clarence Gray Eagle, their uncle, assisted the granddaughters. The Mobridge, South Dakota, Chamber of Commerce also assisted in the disinterment and reburial of Tatanka

Iyotake's remains. The process for moving any person's remains requires the relatives to obtain a disinterment and transfer permit from the state health board. An application for disinterment and transfer permit was submitted as requested by the North Dakota Health Board. The state health officer intervened and stated that Tatanka Iyotake belonged to the state of North Dakota. He was treating Tatanka Iyotake as a piece of property. The health board refused to issue the permit on the state health official's claim. The granddaughters, their uncle, and the Mobridge Chamber of Commerce devised a plan of disinterment. They plotted to enter the cemetery under the cover of darkness and remove Tatanka Iyotake from the Fort Yates military cemetery. The night of April 7, 1953, the plans for removing Tatanka Iyotake began. It started to snow lightly as the gravediggers and the family members, along with the Chamber of Commerce participating members, proceeded to remove the remains. Dan Heupel, a member of the Mobridge Chamber of Commerce, decided to donate to the Chamber of Commerce ten acres of land on the west side of the Missouri River across from Mobridge, South Dakota. He owned fifty acres of land, and the location for the reburial was chosen by the artist Korczak Ziolkowski. (The monument he sculpted is of Nancy Kicking Bear and not the likeness of Tatanka Iyotake.)

Angelique told her children she saw the remains of her grandfather. She said the facial bones were all missing. The bridge of the nose was gone, and there were not any eye sockets. She also said there were pieces of canvas among the remains.

There have been stories told by the One Bull family about the desecration of Tatanka Iyotake's remains. They told of lime being poured on the body and said he was skinned and his skin sold for lampshades. These stories are all false.

119

Angelique Spotted Horse-LaPointe refused to accept the location of the reburial. She stated the people of Standing Rock despised her grandfather and would not take proper care or maintain the new burial site. She made a request to the Rapid City, South Dakota, Chamber of Commerce for assistance in locating a place in the Black Hills for her grandfather to be reinterred. She tried to explain to the members of the Chamber of Commerce about the location of the birthplace of her grandfather, but they chose to ignore her. A reporter said she told him her grandfather's birthplace is at the headwaters of Elk Creek in the Black Hills. The river she referred to is the Yellowstone River in Montana. The Lakota know the Yellowstone River as the Elk River. A small creek branches off the Yellowstone River and used to be Four Horns Creek. This little creek became Pumpkin Creek; this is where Tatanka Iyotake was born. This reporter had doubts about Angelique's story because the Wasicu historians believed the story from Stanley Vestal's book that his birthplace was at a place called Many Caches on the banks of the Grand River at Standing Rock Sioux Reservation. She protested the new location but the other two granddaughters outvoted her.

Her reasons for objecting to this location had been heard, though. The Mobridge Chamber of Commerce and the Standing Rock Sioux Tribe made stipulations in writing: they would care for the gravesite and would not commercialize the area. They proceeded to break the agreement from the very beginning, and this has continued for over fifty-five years. Tatanka Iyotake's burial site is on fee land and not on the Standing Rock Indian Reservation. The white man Dan Heupel, from Mobridge, South Dakota, owned the land.

The gravesite has been in total disarray since 1953. It has always been a party place for the youth from Standing Rock and Mobridge. They have shown their respect through the years by urinating on the monument of Nancy Kicking Bear and trashing the grave with beer bottles and used condoms. This was the reason Angelique LaPointe did not want her grandfather reburied at that location.

Angelique, her husband Claude, and two of her children, Marlene and Ernie, visited the gravesite in 1957 and saw and smelled the condition of her grandfather's burial site. She broke down in tears and told her two children if an opportunity to move the remains of her grandfather ever became available, to do it. This has become an ongoing goal for the descendents of Tatanka Iyotake. The great-grandchildren have plans for the future of Tatanka Iyotake.

LIVING THE LEGACY

Angelique LaPointe taught her children to always respect their great-grandfather. She counseled them to live on their own merits and accomplishments, not on Tatanka Iyotake's name or image. She told her children their great-grandfather was a special person who cared for his people. He suffered for them in the Sun Dance, fought for their survival, and gave everything he had for them, even though he knew they would turn on him and take his life. She said that in the future there would not be another person to equal Tatanka Iyotake's accomplishments for his culture and his people.

She told her children only one person exemplified the generosity, compassion, fortitude, and courage to have the name Tatanka Iyotake. She emphasized to her children not to take the name of her grandfather for themselves or to give the name to their children and grandchildren so they would not disrespect Tatanka Iyotake. The children of Angelique Spotted Horse-LaPointe respected her request and have always been reverent and humble about the image and person of Tatanka Iyotake.

Angelique's children respected her wishes. They were always

modest and did not boast or tell people they were great-grandchildren of Tatanka Iyotake. Friends and neighbors had no idea these quiet humble people had such an important ancestor. It continued this way until the spring of 1992. Then an aunt from the Grey Eagle line took Ernie aside at a meeting and told him it was time for him to come out of the shadows. She told him the people of the Standing Rock Sioux Indian Reservation were capitalizing and commercializing Tatanka Iyotake's name and image. She told him the time had come to reveal to the country and the world that there are lineal descendents of Tatanka Iyotake and to set the record straight. Since some of the men of the

123

Marlene and Ernie at Ernie's home in South Dakota, 2007 (Family photograph)

Lakota Nation still respect the words of elders and women, Ernie took her very seriously.

Ernie and his sister, Ethel, and their aunt, Sarah Spotted Horse-Little Spotted Horse (granddaughter of Tatanka Iyotake), learned of a woman named Betty Butts. Ms. Butts had created a bust of Tatanka Iyotake in bronze and wanted to dedicate it at the Hall of Fame of Indian Chiefs at Anadarko, Oklahoma. Ernie, his sister, and his aunt attended the ceremony. This was the first time people learned of Tatanka Iyotake's lineal descendents. It was the beginning of the journey to set the record straight and to tell the real story of Tatanka Iyotake.

Ernie's sister Marlene gave her power of attorney to her brother to represent her in the issues pertaining to Tatanka Iyotake. As representative of his older sister, Ernie has spent a great deal of time and energy in setting the record straight. He has traveled to other Nations to talk and smoke the pipe, working to heal old enmities. At one point, in the late 1990s, he turned his efforts toward the Standing Rock Sioux tribe.

His wife Sonja's genealogical studies demonstrate that he and his sisters are the only direct descendents of Tatanka Iyotake. That meant that, despite the claims of the One Bull family, there are no direct descendents living on Standing Rock Sioux Reservation, near Tatanka Iyotake's burial site. As descendents of Seen by Her Nation, Ernie and his sisters are all registered members of Pine Ridge Indian Reservation.

Traveling to Standing Rock, Ernie visited the reservation and the tribal offices. In every office he visited, there was a photograph of his great-grandfather. He assumed this was a sign of respect and responded to it warmly. He decided that he would change his enrollment from Pine

Ridge to Standing Rock so that Standing Rock would have a legitimate claim to be the home of Tatanka Iyotake's family. Ernie submitted an application for enrollment at Standing Rock in 1997. A family friend enrolled at the Cheyenne River Indian Reservation applied to transfer his registered membership at the same time.

A short time later, both Ernie and his friend Bill were invited to the offices of the tribal enrollment official at the Standing Rock Sioux tribe. This enrollment official had the responsibility of reviewing all applications for enrollment at the reservation. Ernie, Sonja, and Bill traveled together to this meeting.

For Bill, the matter was simple and his application was approved. To finalize his enrollment, he just had to submit a written request confirming that he wanted to have his membership transferred from the Cheyenne River Indian Reservation to Standing Rock Sioux tribe.

For Ernie, it was not so simple. The tribal council member turned to him and asked,

"And you—why do you want to join the Standing Rock Sioux tribe?"

Ernie explained that he knew there were currently no direct descendents of Tatanka Iyotake at the Standing Rock Sioux Indian Reservation. He was offering to change his enrollment so he could represent the family and the reservation, helping to legitimize their claims to being the home of his great-grandfather. This did not generate the reaction he had expected. The council member replied very negatively, telling him Tatanka Iyotake has *not ever been enrolled at Standing Rock and had no relatives there.* Even further, the council member stated that "Sitting Bull was nothing but a lowly medicine man. He was a coward and a troublemaker."

Shocked, Ernie responded in kind. He pointed out that the tribe certainly had no problem with putting up pictures of the "lowly medicine man" in every office or with claiming him whenever it was to their commercial advantage. The tribal council member's answer was to deny his application for enrollment and to demand that Ernie leave the tribal offices. He threatened to call the tribal police and have Ernie shot. Bill intervened at this point, exclaiming, "So we're going to live 1890 all over again? You're going to have the tribal police shoot him?"

That was when Ernie decided that there would be no way to heal the anger at this time. He has said repeatedly that he is still open to ending the hostility, but it will require an apology from those who have wronged his great-grandfather. When a Lakota takes the life of another Lakota, he is banished from the tribe. If this individual survives the elements and the four-legged, and he returns to the tribe, he returns with gifts to the family of the person he killed. He also will bring a bladder full of water because that is the amount of tears that will be shed. Then he takes the place of the person he killed, but he also is required to take care of his own family. What he did will create a difficult life for this individual for the rest of his life. Most people do not survive after they have been banished.

In those years when the Lakota accepted the role of being Sioux Indians, as in the case of the betrayers of Tatanka Iyotake, they were not banished. What they did is, they cursed their descendants. This curse is four generations long. Their descendants cannot perform the sacred ceremonies nor have a Cannupa that is Wakan. It is simple to ask for forgiveness for what their ancestors did, yet they find it hard to do. Either these people do not know of this curse, or they are just ashamed of their ancestors. The Spirits say these are the people with "Blood on their Hands," and if they do not ask for forgiveness for their ancestors, after the fourth generation is gone, they cannot ever perform the sacred ceremonies. This is one of the reasons the Lakota culture will cease to exist. It has been said, "Before the healing begins, you first have to feel the pain."

127

APPENDIX 1

A Letter from E. D. Mossman, Superintendant of the Standing Rock Indian School, to the Commissioner of Indian Affairs in Washington D.C.

5—1142

DEPARTMENT OF THE INTERIOR Dupt.

UNITED STATES INDIAN FIELD SERVICE
. Standing Rock Indian School,
Fort Yates, North Dakota.

Commissioner of Indian Affairs,
    Washington, D. C.

AUG 25 1922

OFFICE OF INDIAN AFF...
RECEIVED
SEP 5 - 1922
72273

My dear Mr. Commissioner:

I have the honor to reply to the Commissioner's letter of August
10th 1922, which referred to the removal of Sitting Bull's body from
its place of burial in the old Military cemetery at Fort Yates to
some point on the Grand River. With the Commissioner's letter was
a letter from Doane Robinson, Superintendent of the State Historical
Society of South Dakota.

I am very glad that you referred this matter to me before acting
upon it finally, because I feel that it would be a very serious mistake to remove the remains of Sitting Bull from its present resting
place.

Much has been said concerning Sitting Bull, and so much publicity
given to his name and exploits that there is a feeling among the relatives of the policemen, who died in that unfortunate affair, that
too much as already been done in the way of making Sitting Bull a
historical character.

I am not alone in considering him an obstructionist and a demigogue
There is nothing to show that he ever did a single thing constructive
for the Indians, but there is much to show that he kept his ear to the
ground, accommodating his actions and opinions to any movement, which
was against the Government.

His speech when he surrendered to the Government, instead of being the speech of a banquished warrior, or a person who had seen the
error of his ways, but was simply an insulting out burst from a
baffled savage.

I write the above paragraphs as my personal opinion and the
opinion of practically all those who know the conditions under which
this occurrence took place, and who have been conversant with conditions on this reservation since that time.

Should his remains be taken to the Grand River, such an arrange-
ment would arouse old animosities in a degree that I feel sure would
surprise you. As a matter of fact these animosities are not even
slumbering now, but are active. One Elk who owns the land adjoining
the battle ground, periodically makes complaint to the farmer at
Bullhead, that a monument is to be raised on this battle groung to
Sitting Bull and his friends. This always creates considerable,

stir among the Indians and quite often is a subject for a delegation to wait quietly upon me. I have assured them that no action will ever be taken in this matter, if I can prevent it.

There is now at Little Eagle the base of a monument with a sub-base, on which is carved in the Sioux Language these words, "In memory of Sitting Bull and his friends", the shaft to this monument is hidden and no one appears to know where it is. Should this monument be placed on the battle field where it was to be placed, there would be serious trouble. Most of the followers of Sitting Bull are reactionaries, and in talking to Antoine DeRockbraine, who is Farmer at Little Eagle, he told me that if this proposed action were taken the progressive and loyal Indians would consider it a direct slap at them and their progressive ideas and a direct approval of the reactionaries.

I am surprised at the statement in Mr. Robinson's letter to you, when he says that this request is by the relatives of Sitting Bull.

For your information, I will say that Sitting Bull has practic-ally no relatives on this reservation. His nearest of kin now living here are One Bull a nephew and the wife of Grey Eagle. One Bull while his nephew was one of the men who went as police to arrest Sitting Bull at the time of his death. Grey Eagle is a brother in law of Sitting Bull, and while he was not a policeman at the time he was present for the purpose of assisting to arrest Sitting Bull.

After the death of Sitting Bull, his immediate family practically all went to Pine Ridge where his wife number two   and daught-ers and grand children are now living.

In view of the above facts, I hope you will see that this is simply a move by the reactionary element to further their reactionary activities by making a lot of publicity concerning this old Indian, whose only good quality was steadfastness.

His steadfastness apparently never served any good purpose, but was always exerted on the side of reactionaries. He was killed while resisting the authority of the Government. The authorized removal of his remains by his friends would be the subject of a great public spectacle. I recommend that his dust remain where it is and where it should be, in a lonely grave in plain view of the Government school, the Agency buildings and the churches, all of which he fought, until time shall be no more and the trumpet of Gabriel shall sound and call us all before the judgement throne, where Sitting Bull along with the rest of us shall receive his just dues.

Very respectfully,

(E. D. Mossman)
Supt.

EDM:SC
8-18-22

APPENDIX 2

A partial copy of the repatriation document regarding a lock of hair and leggings belonging to Sitting Bull. To view the entire document, please visit the following website:

http://anthropology.si.edu/repatriation/projects/index.htm

Assessment of a Lock of Hair and Leggings Attributed to Sitting Bull, a Hunkpapa Sioux, in the National Museum of Natural History, Smithsonian Institution

William T. Billeck and Betsy Bruemmer

2007

Repatriation Office
Department of Anthropology
National Museum of Natural History
Smithsonian Institution

Executive Summary

In compliance with the National Museum of the American Indian (NMAI) Act of 1989, 20 U.S.C. Section 80q (P.L. 101-185) as amended in 1996 (P.L. 104-278), this report provides an assessment of a lock of hair and leggings attributed to Sitting Bull, a Hunkpapa Sioux, in the collections of the National Museum of Natural History, Smithsonian Institution (Table 1). The lock of hair and leggings were obtained as a loan from Dr. Horace Deeble in 1896. Archival evidence indicates the items were acquired from Sitting Bull's body by Dr. Deeble, an Army Surgeon at Fort Yates in 1890. In 1999, the National Museum of Natural History informed all federally recognized Sioux tribes that a lock of hair and the leggings of Sitting Bull were on loan to the National Museum of Natural History to initiate consultation with the tribes on the items. In 2001, Don Tenoso submitted a request for the repatriation of the lock of hair and leggings. Don Tenoso is a lineal descendant of One Bull, whom he identified as both the nephew and the adopted son of Sitting Bull. In 2002, all of the Sioux tribes were notified of the repatriation request from Don Tenoso and were asked for assistance in locating additional descendants of Sitting Bull. At the same time, three individuals who had been identified as descendants were also notified of the repatriation request. Ernie LaPointe submitted a repatriation request in 2002 along with documentation that there were four living great-grandchildren of Sitting Bull: Ernie LaPointe, Marlene Little Spotted Horse-Anderson, Ethel Little Spotted Horse-Bates, and Lorene Lydia Little Spotted Horse-Red Paint. Marlene Little Spotted Horse-Anderson submitted a power of attorney document allowing Ernie LaPointe to represent her on issues pertaining to Sitting Bull. Ernie LaPointe stated that according to family oral tradition, One Bull was the nephew of Sitting Bull and had not been adopted as Sitting Bull's son, and he would not consider a joint repatriation with the descendants of One Bull. In 2006, Don Tenoso withdrew his repatriation request for the Sitting Bull items because he did not want the separate requests to divide the families.

Table 1. Lock of Hair and Leggings Obtained by Dr. Deeble from Sitting Bull in 1890.

Catalog Number	Description
EL00226	Lock of Hair
EL00227	Leggings

Lineal descendants have the highest standing for making disposition decisions for repatriation under NAGPRA and under the Guidelines and Procedures for Repatriation of the National Museum of Natural History (2006) for the NMAI Act. When lineal descendants can be identified, the closest living generation of descendants has the highest standing and the first priority in making disposition decisions.

The lock of hair and leggings of Sitting Bull were loaned to the museum in 1896. The authority of Dr. Deeble, as a U.S. Army Surgeon, to acquire the lock of hair and leggings is evaluated in this report in order to determine whether the National Museum of Natural History can consider the lock of hair and the leggings to be part of the museum collections. Under U.S. Army regulations in effect at the time, Dr. Deeble, did not have the legal authority to acquire personal items from Sitting Bull's body while employed as an Army Surgeon. In a 2003 letter, Lieutenant Colonel John Patrick of the Office of the Judge Advocate General stated that the Department of the Army had no legal interest in Sitting Bull's lock of hair and leggings. Since Dr. Deeble did not have the legal right to acquire these items and the Department of the Army has no legal interest in the items, the National Museum of Natural History has sufficient possession and control of the lock of hair and leggings to consider a repatriation request. The lock of hair falls under the category of human remains under the NMAI Act and it is recommended that the lock of hair be offered for repatriation to the lineal descendants of Sitting Bull. The leggings do not fall into any of the four categories of items eligible for repatriation under the NMAI Act: human remains, funerary objects, sacred objects and objects of cultural patrimony. However, Dr. Deeble, the collector of the leggings, did not have the legal right to acquire them from Sitting Bull as personal property because they were not obtained with the permission of Sitting Bull or his family at the time that they were acquired. Under long-standing Smithsonian policy, items acquired under circumstances that cast doubt on the validity of the Smithsonian's ownership or possession may be returned to a proper claimant. It is recommended that the leggings be offered for return to lineal descendants of Sitting Bull.

It is recommended that the lock of hair and the leggings be offered for return to the closest living lineal descendants who have requested these items: Sitting Bull's great-grandchildren, Ernie LaPointe and Marlene Little Spotted Horse-Anderson. Ethel Little Spotted Horse-Bates and Lorene Lydia Little Spotted Horse-Red Paint, great-grandchildren of Sitting Bull who have not submitted a repatriation request, will be notified of this decision. In order for the museum to proceed with the return, all individuals of equal standing as closest descendants who have submitted a request for the lock of hair and leggings must be in agreement on the disposition of the items. Don Tenoso and all of the Sioux tribes will also be notified of this recommendation and will be sent a copy of this report. Individuals who have equal or greater standing based on lineal descendance or traditional kinship than the identified great-grandchildren of Sitting Bull should contact William Billeck at the Repatriation Office and provide evidence of their relationship to Sitting Bull if they wish to participate in the disposition decisions. Any new evidence that establishes that a descendant individual has equal or greater standing than the great-grandchildren will be considered by the museum and the evidence may alter the recommendations of this report. Thirty days prior to the return of the lock of hair and leggings, newspaper notices will be placed in regional newspapers to provide public notice to the descendants and to the Sioux people.

Table of Contents

Tables

Appendix

I. Introduction

This report presents the findings and recommendations for a repatriation request from the descendants of Sitting Bull for a lock of hair and cloth leggings that were obtained from Sitting Bull's body shortly after his death. The request is being considered under the repatriation provisions of the NMAI Act of 1989, 20 U.S.C. § 80q (P.L. 101-185), as amended in 1996 (P.L. 104-278), and under the collection policy of the Smithsonian. The NMAI Act requires the Smithsonian Institution to inventory and identify the tribal origins of all Native American human remains currently in its possession. Culturally identifiable human remains are to be expeditiously returned to the culturally affiliated federally recognized tribe or lineal descendant upon their request. In compliance with this law, the Repatriation Office prepared this report to evaluate and document the affiliation of the lock of hair. The leggings, as described in the following report, do not fit the repatriation object categories of funerary object, sacred object, or object of cultural patrimony and have been evaluated under the Smithsonian collection policy.

The findings of this report are based on the National Museum of Natural History's master computer catalog, correspondence sent to the museum by the original collectors, Department of Anthropology ledger books, catalog card files, original accession documents, reports, historical documents, publications, military records, and information provided by descendants of Sitting Bull.

The report is divided into five sections. Following the introduction, Section II presents an overview of the history of the repatriation request. Section III reviews how the lock of hair and leggings were obtained and loaned to the Smithsonian and describes the items. Section IV assesses the status of the lock of hair and leggings as a loan, evaluates the repatriation categories for the lock of hair and leggings, reviews the evidence that has been assembled on descendants of Sitting Bull, and identifies the closest living Sitting Bull descendants that are known to the museum. The final part, Section V, summarizes the findings of this report and provides recommendations.

Overview of Lineal Descendant Requests

Under the NMAI Act and the NAGPRA, lineal descendants, federally recognized tribes and Native Hawaiian organizations have the right to make repatriation requests for human remains and certain categories of objects. Lineal descendants are given the highest standing for making disposition decisions for repatriation of human remains and certain categories of objects under NAGPRA and under the Guidelines and Procedures for Repatriation of the National Museum of Natural History (2006). When lineal descendants can be identified, they have the sole responsibility for making disposition decisions and their decisions take precedence over the decisions of more remote descendants. When lineal descendants cannot be identified, the affiliated federally recognized tribe(s) or Native Hawaiian organization has the responsibility for making disposition decisions.

When lineal descendants can be identified, and objects or human remains have been found to fit a repatriation category, the closest living generation of descendants that have submitted a request have the highest standing and the first priority for making disposition decisions. All of the individuals within a generation of descendants have equal standing. For instance, all grandchildren that make a request have equal standing and that standing supercedes that of great-grandchildren. In this case, only the grandchildren would make disposition decisions and the great-grandchildren would have no role in the decisions unless the descendants with standing determined that they should be included in the disposition decisions. In order for a repatriation to proceed, all individuals that have *made a request* and have equal standing must agree on the disposition of the remains and/or objects. Known descendants who have not made a request and are of equal standing to those who have made a request will be notified by the museum of the intention to return the remains and/or objects and provided an opportunity to submit a request.

II. History of the Repatriation Request

In August of 1999, Chuck Smythe of the National Museum of Natural History Repatriation Office wrote to the representatives of the Sioux tribes to inform them that the museum held leggings and a lock of hair attributed to Sitting Bull. The following tribes were informed: Standing Rock Sioux Tribe, Oglala Sioux Tribe, Rosebud Sioux Tribe, Lower Brule Sioux, Crow Creek Sioux, Cheyenne River Sioux, Yankton Sioux Tribe, Flandreau Santee Sioux Tribe, Ft. Peck Sioux Tribe, Upper Sioux Indian Community, Shakopee Mdewakanton Sioux Community, Prairie Island Indian Community, Lower Sioux Indian Community, Santee Sioux Tribe, Spirit Lake Nation, and the Sisseton Wahpeton Sioux. Smythe explained that these items were not included in the ethnographic summary reports sent out in 1996 because the items were on loan to the museum. As it appears that the items were acquired without permission from the family of Sitting Bull, the Repatriation Office wished to consult with the Sioux tribes. Chuck Smythe left the Repatriation Office at the end of 2000, and William Billeck was assigned the responsibility to respond to inquiries on the Sitting Bull items.

The only response to the notification came on February 24, 2001, when Don Tenoso submitted a request for the repatriation of Sitting Bull's lock of hair and leggings. He identified Henry Oscar One Bull as the son of Sitting Bull's sister and as the adopted son of Sitting Bull through *Hunka*, the making of relatives. During a visit with William Billeck on February 26, 2001, Don Tenoso identified himself as the great-grandson of Henry Oscar One Bull and through adoption, as the great-great-grandson of Sitting Bull. One Bull was Sitting Bull's nephew (sister's son) and was not a biological lineal descendant. Don Tenoso wrote that:

> ... One Bull is the 'son' of Sitting Bull. The term
> 'son' is used to define the relationship between
> One Bull and Sitting Bull, because Sitting Bull
> 'adopted' (a modern US term), '*Hunka*' (Lakota
> term meaning the making of relative) One Bull
> at a very early age from Sitting Bull's sister [Don
> Tenoso to William Billeck, letter, February 24, 2001,
> italics added].

On April 24, 2001, William Billeck informed Don Tenoso that the museum would assemble a list of close descendants of Sitting Bull to notify of the request. Don Tenoso was asked to submit the names of any descendants that he thought should be notified of

139
◈

the request. The museum also would notify all of the Sioux tribes that a request for repatriation had been received. On November 29, 2001, Ron Little Owl, then a member of the Smithsonian's Native American Repatriation Review Committee and a member of the Three Affiliated Tribes of North Dakota, told William Billeck that Ernie LaPointe, Ethel Little Spotted Horse-Bates, and Marlene Little Spotted Horse-Anderson were lineal descendants of Sitting Bull. On February 22, 2002, all of the federally recognized Sioux tribes and the three individuals reported to be close lineal descendants of Sitting Bull were notified that a request had been received for the repatriation of the Sitting Bull items. The following tribes were informed: Standing Rock Sioux Tribe, Oglala Sioux Tribe, Rosebud Sioux Tribe, Lower Brule Sioux, Crow Creek Sioux, Cheyenne River Sioux, Yankton Sioux Tribe, Flandreau Santee Sioux Tribe, Ft. Peck Sioux Tribe, Upper Sioux Indian Community, Shakopee Mdewakanton Sioux Community, Prairie Island Indian Community, Lower Sioux Indian Community, Santee Sioux Tribe, Spirit Lake Nation, and the Sisseton Wahpeton Sioux. The notification also asked for assistance in locating additional lineal descendants of Sitting Bull.

140
◇

On February 27, 2002, Ernie LaPointe sent an email to William Billeck expressing an interest in the Sitting Bull items. In a February 28, 2002, phone call Ernie LaPointe repeated that he was interested in repatriating the Sitting Bull items and also said that they should not be returned to the descendants of One Bull. Ernie LaPointe sent a letter dated March 4, 2002, containing a kinship chart that showed that Ernie LaPointe and his three sisters, Ethel Little Spotted Horse- Bates, Marlene Little Spotted Horse-Anderson and Lorene Lydia Little Spotted Horse-Red Paint, were the closest living lineal descendants of Sitting Bull. The email, phone call, and letter were interpreted as a repatriation request by the Repatriation Office. The March 4, 2002, letter also stated that One Bull was a nephew and was not an adopted son of Sitting Bull. On July 22, 2003, William Billeck traveled to Lead, South Dakota to meet with Ernie LaPointe, Ethel Little Spotted Horse-Bates, and others to discuss evidence pertaining to the repatriation case. At this meeting, Ernie LaPointe said that he wished to request the Sitting Bull items and that the items should not be returned to the One Bull descendants. According to family tradition as described by Ernie LaPointe, One Bull was the nephew of Sitting Bull and had not been adopted as a son by him. Ernie LaPointe stated that the *Hunka* was for the making of a relative, and the ceremony would not have been used for an individual who already was a relative. Ernie LaPointe went on to identify One Bull as the nephew of Sitting Bull, and said that since One Bull was already a relative, he could not have been adopted as a relative through the *Hunka*. Ernie LaPointe stated that he was not willing to consider a joint repatriation with the descendants of One Bull because they were not lineal descendants and because One Bull had not been adopted by Sitting Bull. On September 27, 2005, Ernie LaPointe, Joseph Tiona, and Sonja LaPointe visited the museum to examine the Sitting Bull items. On December 12, 2005, Don Tenoso met with William Billeck to discuss the repatriation request and at the end of the meeting Don Tenoso said he planned to phone Ernie LaPointe. The next day, Ernie LaPointe phoned William Billeck and said that Don Tenoso was withdrawing his request. Don Tenoso reported that he was withdrawing his request in a phone call to William Billeck on December 14, 2005. He said that he would send a written notice of the withdrawal on December 15, 2005, and that he did not want the separate requests to divide the families. Don Tenoso repeated his intention to withdraw the request in phone conversations on January 13, 2006, and February 9, 2006.

On March 15, 2006, William Billeck wrote to Don Tenoso to inform him that his request would withdrawn based on the December 14, 2005, phone call, unless he responded otherwise in writing by April 15, 2006. On April 10, 2006, Don Tenoso left a phone message for William Billeck and asked to have an extension to the end of the April in order to prepare a letter to withdraw the request. William Billeck called Don Tenoso and left a phone message on April 12, 2006, agreeing to an extension of the date to April 30, 2006. During an April 20, 2007, phone call, Don Tenoso asked for a copy of the records on how the Sitting Bull items had been acquired so that he could write the letter to withdraw the request. He said that he was going to Standing Rock to attend the meeting on the proposed moving of Sitting Bull's grave from near Mobridge, South Dakota, to the Little Big Horn National Monument. On April 23, 2007, copies of the records were sent to Don Tenoso. As of June 2007, Don Tenoso has not sent a letter withdrawing or reinstating his request, but based on his phone call of December 15, 2005 and his failure to reinstate the request by April 30, 2006, his request for the Sitting Bull items is considered withdrawn.

On February 23, 2006, William Billeck called Ernie LaPointe to ask him to clarify the repatriation request made in the email of February 27, 2002, the phone call of February 28, 2002, l, and the letter of March 4, 2002, in which he expressed interest in the Sitting Bull items. Ernie LaPointe sent a letter on February 23, 2006, requesting the lock of hair and leggings. The letter also included a power of attorney document, dated September 6, 2005, from his sister, Marlene Little Spotted Horse-Anderson, designating Ernie LaPointe her representative on issues pertaining to Sitting Bull. This report will only evaluate the lineal descendant request of Ernie LaPointe and Marlene Little Spotted Horse-Anderson.

142
◇

GLOSSARY

Cannupa	*sacred pipe*
Hanblecheyapi	*vision quest*
Hunkayapi	*making of a relative ceremony*
Hunkesni	*slow moving, weak, sickly*
Inipi	*purification ceremony (sweat lodge)*
Itazipco	*whiteout bows*
Kangi Siha	*Crowfoot*
Maza Zee	*gold ore*
Minneconjou	*planters near the water*
Oglala	*Scatter Among Themselves*
Oohenumpa	*Two Kettle*
Sicangu	*Burned Thighs*
Sihasapa	*Blackfoot*
Ta Oyate Wanyankopi Win	*Seen By Her Nation Woman*
Ta Sina Topa Win	*Four Robes Woman or Four Blanket Woman*
Tasiyagnupa	*meadowlark*
Tatanka Iyotake	*Buffalo Bull Who Sits Down*
Tatanka Psica	*Buffalo Bull Who Jumps*
Tatanka Wansila	*Buffalo Bull Who Is One*
Tatanka Wi Uha Naji	*Buffalo Bull Stands With His Woman*

Ti Tanen Win	*Lodge In Sight Woman*
Tiatunwa	*looking for a homesite*
Tiyospaye	*extended family*
Tunkashila	*grandfather*
Wakan	*sacred, holy*
Wakan Icaga	*something scared is growing (children)*
Wakan Tanka	*Great Spirit*
wakapa pi	*pounded dried meat*
Wakayaja	*something scared is growing (children)—* *a short version of Wakan Icaga*
Wasicu	*American*
Watanya Cikala	*Little Sure Shot*
Wicasa	*man*
Wicasa Wakan	*holy man/medicine man*
Wiwang Wacipi	*Gazing at the Sun (Sun Dance)*
Wiyakewaste Win	*Good Feather Woman*
Wovoka	*Paiute Holy Man, aka Jack Wilson*

∽

Ernie LaPointe, a great-grandson of Sitting Bull, was born on the Pine Ridge Indian Reservation in South Dakota. He is a Sun Dancer who lives the traditional way of the Lakota and follows the rules of the sacred pipe. LaPointe and his wife, Sonja, live in South Dakota.